T0303931

David Collins has succeeded where few others have. He has written a book on the power of storytelling in management that is readable, critical and provocative. It is a book that will enlighten and stimulate practicing managers, students and scholars. But the highest praise for the author is that in doing all this he has told a powerful story in its own right. And he has told it brilliantly.

Yiannis Gabriel, Professor, University of Bath, UK

Stories for Management Success

We tend to assume that we may divide our activities into talk and action. In so doing we tend to suggest that talk is subordinate to action.

Taking issue with these presumptions, *Stories for Management Success: The Power of Talk in Organizations* argues that talk is central to what managers do. Indeed it argues that, for managers, 'walking the walk' necessarily implies 'talking the talk such that storytelling is now central to managerial work'. Noting that managerial talk is increasingly located within an account of storytelling the book offers a critical review of the academic debates associated with telling tales at work and uses this critical reflection to shape and guide those who would realise the power of talk. Thus, the book concludes with six key questions designed to prompt both introspection and action on storytelling in an organized context. With reflections on the relevant management research, the author provides a scholar's digest to aid management thinking and practice.

This book offers an examination of the processes of organizational storytelling and has been designed to allow practitioners of management to recognise and in so doing to unleash the power of talk in organizations.

David Collins is Professor in Management and Dean of the Suffolk Business School, University of Suffolk (UK). A graduate of the universities of Glasgow, Strathclyde and Essex, David is British by birth and Scottish by the Grace of God. This is his fourth book published by Routledge.

Routledge Focus on Business and Management

The fields of business and management have grown exponentially as areas of research and education. This growth presents challenges for readers trying to keep up with the latest important insights. *Routledge Focus on Business and Management* presents small books on big topics and how they intersect with the world of business.

Individually, each title in the series provides coverage of a key academic topic, whilst collectively, the series forms a comprehensive collection across the business disciplines.

For a complete list of titles in this series, please visit www.routledge.com/business/series/FBM

Manager vs. Leader: Untying the Gordian Knot
Robert M. Murphy and Kathleen M. Murphy

Accounting for Biological Assets
Rute Goncalves and Patricia Teixeira Lopes

Rising Consumer Materialism
A Threat to Sustainable Happiness
Afia Khalid and Faisal Qadeer

Evaluating IT Projects
Eriona Shtembari

Ethics, Meaning, and Market Society
Laszlo Zsolnai

Stories for Management Success
The Power of Talk in Organizations
David Collins

How to Resolve Conflict in Organizations
The Power of People Models and Procedure
Annamaria Garden

Stories for Management Success
The Power of Talk in Organizations

David Collins

Routledge
Taylor & Francis Group

LONDON AND NEW YORK

First published 2018
by Routledge
2 Park Square, Milton Park, Abingdon, Oxon OX14 4RN

and by Routledge
711 Third Avenue, New York, NY 10017

Routledge is an imprint of the Taylor & Francis Group, an informa business

© 2018 David Collins

British Library Cataloguing in Publication Data
A catalogue record for this book is available from the British Library

Library of Congress Cataloging in Publication Data
A catalog record has been requested for this book

ISBN: 978-1-138-06246-7 (hbk)
ISBN: 978-1-315-16160-0 (ebk)

Typeset in Times New Roman
by Taylor & Francis Books

Made in Kilmarnock

Contents

List of illustrations

Figure

Boxes

1 Introduction

In everyday conversational exchange we generally employ forms of speech which privilege certain types of behaviour. In so doing, however, we tend to denigrate other modes of conduct. As a child, for example, I can recall being told that I was 'a chatterbox'. Furthermore I was given to understand that having been labelled in this way I was obliged to do something about it. Indeed I soon learned that *at the very least* I should 'shut up' so that the adults and the less talkative children around me could get on with *doing* something useful.

Of course it was not just children who were subject to such forms of (linguistic) discipline: The adults, I now realise, also lived in a world where 'talk was cheap' and to be 'a gossip' was a great insult that carried very real social repercussions.

In this text I intend to build upon these childhood reflections. My aim is to produce analytical insights on the 'talk' and 'action' which in so many ways shape and construct our endeavours. Through this I hope to prompt introspection on the processes of management and, perhaps more importantly, I hope to promote useful forms of managerial action which appreciate the significance of organizational storytelling *and* the power of talk in this dynamic context.

Huczynski is one of a number of scholars who have devoted their careers to the study of management and managing (see for example Huczynski and Buchanan 2007). In the early 1990s he produced a notable study which examines the work of management's gurus. Discussing the deeper structure of 'guru theory' Huczynski (1993) argues that seemingly diverse forms of guru theorising share and project common presumptions about the nature of work and the processes of managing (see also Grint 1994). Probing these similarities Huczynski suggests that management's gurus embed their offerings within narrative frameworks that threaten and yet reaffirm the status of the managerial leader. Pattison (1997) and Jackson (1996; 2001) echo and expand upon this point. Discussing Tom Peters' (1988) *Thriving on Chaos*, for example, Pattison suggests that this text amounts to a secular retelling of the biblical tale of Noah. Thus Pattison argues that *Thriving on Chaos* builds upon a narrative which threatens *each of us* with a deluge (of foreign competition) yet promises salvation to those who are willing to construct an ark (designed according to the parameters of 'chaos' and 'excellence' as outlined by Peters).

Recognising that contemporary management has been constructed in and through narratives, this little book focuses upon the medium used to persuade us that managing is, at root, a 'moral project' (Watson 2001). To this end we offer an extended analysis and review of a special form of managerial talk known more commonly as organizational storytelling. I do not, you will note, suggest that organizational storytelling constitutes a management fashion that is to be dismissed or derided as somehow faddish and ephemeral. Instead I will argue that organizational storytelling needs to be taken seriously. Indeed, I will argue that stories act to structure thinking and action within organizations and are, therefore, central to managerial success.

Yet I will also suggest that practitioners of management have been exposed only to 'sensegiving' perspectives (Collins 2013) which assert that organizational storytelling offers a relatively simple means of advancing managerial control. To counter this unhelpful assumption I will offer reflections on 'talk' and 'action' in managerial work (see Marshak 1998) which highlight the importance of 'sensemaking' processes (Weick 1995). This text, therefore, will argue that the denigration of 'talk' has continued into my adult life and extends beyond the Kilmarnock streets that shaped my formative years. Indeed I will suggest that 'talk' in the field of business and management has been, variously, denied, devalued and distorted.

Challenging the disciplinary assumptions that shape our appreciation of *real* managerial work, I will insist that the business of management is, in fact, founded upon persuasive *talk*. Recognising the reproach that is contained within the familiar challenge: *You talk the talk but can you walk the walk?* I will argue that, for practitioners of management, this all too familiar censure needs to be recognised as wrong-headed *and* counter-productive because it suggests that action and talk may be separated. Furthermore I will argue that those who would separate action and talk misunderstand the essence of managerial work because they tend to assert that talk is, in fact, subordinate to action. Countering the reproof voiced above, therefore, I will argue that managers are tested, daily, and when tested need to develop and demonstrate their capabilities in and through *talk*. Recognising the demands of this regime, I will argue that the special form of talk known as organizational storytelling holds the key to management success. Overturning the presumptions that devalue *talk* and which would subordinate talk to action, therefore, I will argue that in organized contexts, walking the walk necessarily implies talking the talk!

In an attempt to situate this analysis within a context which enables action and yet appreciates the plurality and the complexity of organized settings I will offer what I have, elsewhere, termed 'critical-practical' (Collins 2000) insights on the practice of storytelling. This critical-practical approach, as we shall see, has been developed so that you, the reader, might take steps to reflect upon and, perhaps more importantly, to improve your storytelling practice.

Accordingly the text is structured as follows: In Chapter 2 I begin with brief reflections on the nature of management. Texts prepared for practising managers seldom look critically at the nature of managerial work. This is regrettable because critical perspectives on management and managing offer, as we shall learn, useful insights on the problems, processes and dilemmas which arise as we seek to work with and through others.

Noting that 'management' is normally framed in terms of outputs, our critical review will counter that 'managing' is more usefully conceptualised as a social and political process which, while it is founded upon 'persuasion', is enacted in settings that often make it rather difficult to get people *to do things*. Recognising the central role which 'persuasion' and indeed emotion perform in the managerial process, Chapter 3 will consider attempts which have been made to locate managerial work within an account of storytelling.

While noting that managerial work has been usefully framed as a narrative endeavour, Chapter 3 will, nonetheless, suggest that our appreciation of the organizational processes which shape and construct managerial work remains rooted in sensegiving models of storytelling. Contrasting such sensegiving accounts with an alternative framed by Weick's (1995) account of sensemaking, we will attempt to situate and redeem the social and political complexities which have been, too often, ignored within the analysis of organizational storytelling.

Chapter 4 builds upon this account of the contest between sensegiving and sensemaking as it examines, more closely, the academic debates which structure our appreciation of stories and storytelling. Chapter 4 will, therefore, reflect upon the different ways in which stories might be defined and acted upon. Here we will probe the different ways in which 'reports', 'opinions' and 'stories' seek to construct and account for events. In addition we will examine the division between 'deductive' and 'inductive' accounts of storytelling (Collins 2013). Chapter 4 will also analyse the tools which storytellers may call upon as they attempt to shape our appreciation of the world and its problems. To allow readers to put these reflections to work we will offer a *pro forma* designed to reveal the different ways in which epic, comic, romantic and tragic tales deploy narrative resources.

Chapter 4, as we shall, see is rich with stories and indulges a little meandering. Yet our meanders have a purpose because the tales which mark this (water) course have been selected and/or designed to enhance your appreciation of the ways in which storytellers can intervene in sensible environments, variously, framing events and forming characters as they attempt to shape thought and action. Chapter 5 builds directly upon these tales and offers a number of key questions designed to enliven both talk and action. Chapter 5, therefore, will offer six questions designed to precipitate reflection on your storytelling practices so that you might (a) understand the power of talk, and (b) put storytelling to work within your own organization. Finally Chapter 6 will offer a brief summary of our analysis and concluding comments designed to cement your appreciation of the role(s) which stories perform in successful managerial endeavours.

2 Managerial work

What do managers do?

For many readers this question will, I presume, sound like the sort of interrogation that announces a joke. I know lots of jokes about management consultants but for some reason I do not seem to know any good jokes about managers. I could, however, begin this analysis of organizational storytelling with a joke, for there are clear narrative similarities between jokes and stories: Both place actors in a scene and then outline an interaction between events, the actors and the situation, which proceeds to a conclusion that – in the case of the joke – is designed to generate laughter. In addition it is worth observing that, beyond precipitating the physical response of laughter, jokes, like stories, may serve to illustrate and, in so doing, may challenge the sensibilities of the audience (see Double 2005; Lee 2010). Indeed, if we are very fortunate jokes, like stories, may also tell us something more generally about the human condition.[1] I will not, however, pursue an approach based upon joking within this text. There are two reasons for this. First, as I mentioned before I do not seem to know any good gags about managing. And second, I want to make sure that my point is taken seriously.[2]

Joking aside, then, the issue as I see it is that through some unfortunate confluence of habit and tuition we tend to conceptualise management in ways which deny its complexity. Furthermore we indulge codifications which overwrite our intuitive appreciation of the dynamics of social organization (Chia and King 1998). Thus we tend to depict organizations as *things*; as stable institutions. And having assumed that we can treat organizations as entities we then represent managing as a simple, linear, matter of cause and effect (Czarniawska 1997; 1999).

Consider for a moment your own curriculum vitae. My guess is that it will focus upon what you have done (*because talk is cheap*) and it will, furthermore, contain declarations which take personal credit for key outcomes (*because you need to demonstrate that you can walk the walk*):

> I delivered a 22% improvement in output ... a 17% improvement in profitability ... year-on-year increases in labour productivity ... a 47% reduction in waste ... a 74% increase in un-read memos.

This outcome, or output-focused, account of management is, I concede, perfectly legitimate at some level. For example I expect the companies and agencies that I am obliged to interact with to *do* things for me. And I will acknowledge that, nowadays, I expect these things to be done rather quickly. Furthermore when I participate in selection interviews I expect that the candidates will be able to show me what they can do.

Yet the problem with this outcome-oriented, cause-and-effect, account of management is that it tends to obscure the ways in which managers actually get things done. Academics and academic institutions must take some of the blame for this state of affairs because in a desire to bring some degree of shape and order to the shifting, dynamic and complex business of managing others we have indulged codifications which project a narrow action-orientation. Following Fayol (1949), therefore, those who teach 'management' typically tell students that managers *plan, organize, command, control* and *co-ordinate* the actions of others. Moreover those of us who teach 'management' tend to talk at length about the types of activity associated with these tasks. Yet we say much less about the practical problems; the social and political issues that arise when we seek to plan, organize and control the thoughts and actions of others.

We do not need, however, to indulge these codifications when we teach or, more generally, when we talk about the processes of managing. In a small-scale but highly influential study Mintzberg (1973), for example, provides a useful appreciation of the day-to-day problems and dilemmas of managerial work. Analysing the everyday activities that managers undertake, Mintzberg reminds us that these agents are situated in complex hierarchies. We have, as you well know, first-line managers, middle managers and senior managers. These practitioners, no matter whether they are senior production managers or middle ranking facilities managers, we should note, operate in dynamic contexts that are prone to change. Recognising this, Mintzberg warns us that managing is inherently political. Managers, he tells us, are obliged to spend a large part of their working lives actively negotiating the boundaries of their own discretion and responsibility. Indeed he suggests that the daily problems of co-ordinating others – and we might add, controlling yourself – are such that managers must spend rather a lot of their working lives in meetings. Mintzberg adds that, when they are in such gatherings, managers must engage in forms of conversational exchange that are – to a greater or lesser degree – designed to engage people in forms of thought and action that they might otherwise choose not to pursue. These otherwise avoided activities might include getting up early to travel to a meeting; making just one more sales call; or even reading this little book!

Yet whatever your reason for reading this book, Mintzberg's study should serve to remind us that, despite the familiar codifications, managing others and yourself is, at root, a social-political process hinged upon the arts of persuasion. This expression, as we shall see, reflects an understanding that managerial control – the ability to shape the thoughts and actions of others – is incomplete. We should add, moreover, that it is often self-defeating.

Why might managerial control be considered to be both incomplete and potentially self-defeating?

The short answer is that while the familiar codifications of management imply a fixation with 'command' and 'control', work within simple and indeed more complex organizations necessarily implies co-operation such that the whole history of managing (see for example Bendix [1956] 1963; Thompson [1963] 1972; Ramsay 1977; Zuboff 1988; Hales 1993; Collins 1997; Marchington 2005) might be said to boil down to a search for forms of co-ordination that do not break down or otherwise intrude upon the social co-operation that *gets things done*. Despite Fayol's (1949) codification, therefore, it is worth pointing out that control (albeit fragile in nature and temporary in its effectiveness) is not the primary concern of the organizational elite that guides our agencies and corporations. Control may well be *a means* to the end that managers seek, but the organizational end – as we saw when we dipped into our CVs – will not be control *per se*. The end that is sought will be output, or productivity, or growth, or profitability ... or all three simultaneously.

Edwards (1986) captures these tensions rather well. Reflecting upon the nature of the employment relationship, Edwards observes that 'labour' is quite unlike the other factors of production conventionally recognised in the study of economics. Thus Edwards observes that while we can simply purchase tracts of land and quantities of capital we cannot do the same with labour. Instead we are obliged to purchase 'labour power'; a capacity to work. The problem being, of course, that since most of us are paid simply to attend work the capacity of labour power to do something useful – something profitable – may go unrealised. Recognising this indeterminacy, those who manage labour power are, Edwards suggests, obliged to find ways to direct and to control what their employees and co-workers do. Yet since employment is an exchange relationship employees have an incentive to resist their employers' attempts either to extend or to intensify their work activity. This implies that the parties to the employment relationship must address a fundamental conflict because their economic interests are divergent. Indeed this gap between the needs of the parties to the contract suggests that the employment relationship is, potentially, antagonistic. Moreover we would do well to note that this conflict potential is built into the very foundations of the relationship. Drawing these points together Edwards (1986) suggests that the employment relationship is founded upon, and may be considered to be, a 'structured antagonism'.

This conceptualisation of the employment relationship as a 'structured antagonism' often angers or unsettles practising managers. These individuals tend to utilise unitary (Fox 1985) models of organization, and so, draw upon metaphors which highlight teamworking and common goals when they are invited to discuss their management philosophies (Ramsay 1975; Harvey-Jones 1994). It is worth making the point explicitly, therefore, that to accept that the employment relationship is, at root, a structured antagonism does not necessarily imply that managers are nasty and exploitative. Clearly some managers *are* pretty nasty and fairly exploitative. John DeLorean for example (Wright 1980) seems to have been a tragically vain individual with criminal tendencies. Harold Geneen was, at least according to some accounts (see Geneen and Moscow 1986), a playground bully. And Al Dunlap (Dunlap and Andelman 1997) was, I suggest, a weapons grade monster. But in my experience most managers are pretty decent specimens of humanity. It is therefore important to be clear about the implications which flow from the analysis offered by Edwards (1986). Thus to suggest that the employment relationship is constituted upon a structured antagonism is simply to observe that those who have something to sell, whether this is second-hand cars, designer sunglasses or labour power have a clear and personal interest in brokering the best deal available. Those who seek to purchase goods and services, however, have an interest in obtaining these as cheaply as possible. Consequently both parties to the contract of employment must find some way either to close or to regulate the gap that persists between their needs and the expectations of others.

Yet it is also important to note that the contract of employment is not simply an economic exchange. The contract of employment is not simply an agreement on the price of labour. It is, if you care to look carefully, also a document that traces and expresses the social and political controls which shape our actions within and beyond the workplace. Discussing Britain's Industrial Revolution, for example, E. P. Thompson (1967) documents the development of a complex penal code designed to outlaw and to punish certain forms of conduct deemed to be undesirable in the workplace. Indeed, Thompson observes that what we would now call the staff handbook for the workers employed by the Etruria pottery ran to some 500 pages as it documented the punishments consequent upon organizational misbehaviour.

Weighing the merits of the 'five dollar day' which was implemented by Henry Ford, Beynon (1979) draws our attention to the broader social controls that employers have attempted to enforce within the contract of employment. Thus Beynon observes that Ford paid this very attractive daily rate only to those employees who had received a favourable report from the 'sociological department' on their family lives and on their broader personal habits!

Hopefully it should now be clear that the general tendency to equate management with control needs to be understood in the context of attempts to shape and direct a relationship of exchange which, because it is indeterminate, carries with it a very clear conflict-potential. Yet while conceding this point it is also important to point out that while controlling and directing the activity of others is indeed a large part of what many managers find themselves doing on a day-to-day basis, the impulse to control may undermine the economic ends – profitability, productivity, etc. – which organizations are, when all is said and done, constituted to pursue. Why should this be so?

The answer to this question is, perhaps, deceptively simple: Management control is limited and potentially self-defeating because policies designed to advance or secure control tend to undermine the co-operation, the adaptation, the imagination and, indeed, the spontaneity that solves problems, develops products and opens markets. And why do we find ourselves in circumstances where the exercise of control subverts the desire to get things done through and with others? Again the answer is simple: The more a contract of employment attempts to specify directly, concretely and in advance of the situation what it is that employees are expected to do at any point in time, the more that contract will provide a license for individuals and groups to respond: *You can't tell me to do that, that's not my job. That's not in my contract!*

Bendix [1956] (1963) captures this rather well. In a classic and often-cited passage he offers the following observation on the nature and limitations of managerial control:

Management no matter how expert, cannot set out in advance exactly what must be done under all circumstances and how, but must rely to some extent on the workers' co-operation, initiative and experience.

(256)

Recognising that attempts to impose direct forms of control within the employment relationship are self-limiting, managers have, in recent decades, attempted to shift our common-sense understanding of the relationship of employment *from* a conflict-laden, legal-economic exchange, *to* a moral project. Thus much of modern management practice has retreated from direct control mechanisms and has, instead, focused upon narrative frameworks which assert that the parties to the employment relationship are agreed on organizational ends *and* means because all recognise that their mutual prosperity depends upon vanquishing competitors and satisfying customers.

Returning to the question that we started with – what do managers do? – it should now be apparent that modern managers are centrally concerned with talk, not because they are chatty by nature, but because the nature of the employment relationship itself means that those who have responsibility for the work that is undertaken by others are obliged to produce persuasive rhetorics that will convince colleagues, employees, shareholders and stakeholders that they are engaged in endeavours which are, in any sense, worthy.

So one more time: What do managers do? They plan; they organize; they command; they control; and they co-ordinate, of course. But it is purposeful talk that causes and allows all of these processes. It is talk that persuades people to smile at the customer; to work hard; to stay late; and to write books!

It is talk, we would do well to observe, that lifts our gaze from the vulgarities of economic exchange to embrace the nobilities of vision, purpose and mission. It is talk that makes work emotional. It is talk that gets us up in the morning. It is talk that keeps us moving. It is talk, in short, which animates and orientates (De Cock and Hipkin 1997).

In our next section we will look more closely at the purposeful talk which is at the heart of modern managerial projects as we consider the nature of organizational storytelling.

Notes

1 Cathcart and Klein (2007) would endorse and yet extend this point. They suggest that jokes and philosophy share core concerns and orientations:

'The construction and payoff of jokes and the construction and payoff of philosophical concepts are made out of the same stuff. They tease the mind in similar ways. That's because philosophy and jokes proceed from the same impulse: to confound our sense of the way things are, to flip our worlds upside down and to ferret out hidden, often uncomfortable, truths about life. What the philosopher calls and insight, the gagster calls a zinger' (2).

2 I will, however, make a more concerted attempt to make you laugh at later points!

3   Organizational storytelling

Our appreciation of what managers do is, nowadays, routinely located in 'talk'. Furthermore the purposeful 'talk' which is said to be central to managerial success has been structured, increasingly, as a form of storytelling. The reasons for this change are, in truth, complex and potentially contestable. But this is *my* book, and since I do not have the time or indeed the space to mess around I will offer, briefly, *my* reflections on the factors which, *as I see it*, have acted to underpin this development.

As I see it the roots of our contemporary interest in organizational storytelling may be traced to two books which were published in the early 1980s. These books, *The Art of Japanese Management* co-authored by Pascale and Athos ([1981] 1986), and *In Search of Excellence* which was produced by Peters and Waterman (1982) share a number of features. Both texts were produced in the context of an American economy which had been rocked by double-digit rates of unemployment, inflation and banking interest. In addition both texts recognised that some of America's competitors seemed to be immune to such problems. Indeed, it is worth conceding that both texts recognised that while America had become mired in recession the Japanese economy had continued to grow and, in market after market, had come to challenge American producers. Capturing the scale of this challenge, Pascale and Athos (1986: 20) offered the following observation:

> In 1980 Japan's GNP was third highest in the world and if we extrapolate current trends it would be number one by the year 2000. A country the size of Montana, Japan has virtually no physical resources, yet it supports over 115 million people (half the population of the United States), exports $75 billion worth more goods than it imports and has an investment rate as well as a GNP

growth rate which is twice that of the United States. Japan has come to dominate in one selected industry after another – eclipsing the British in motorcycles, surpassing the Germans and the Americans in automobile production, wrestling leadership from the Germans and the Swiss in watches, cameras and optical instruments and overcoming the United States' historical dominance in businesses as diverse as steel, shipbuilding, pianos, zippers and consumer electronics.

Reflecting upon the roots of this economic success, Pascale and Athos suggested that Japan's growing dominance was, primarily, managerial. Japanese managers, the authors argued, had successfully tapped into the emotions of their employees and in so doing had secured employee commitment to customers, to innovation and to change. Pursuing this distinctive managerial capability, both Pascale and Athos, and Peters and Waterman, utilised the McKinsey 7-S framework (see Figure 3.1) and in so doing argued that American managers needed to rebalance the hard-S factors and the soft-S factors of business in order to ensure that America corporations would have cultures appropriate to the business needs of the 1980s and beyond.

Yet despite these very clear similarities only one of these books has enjoyed broad commercial success. It is worth pausing to consider the differing fortunes of these otherwise remarkably similar texts.

In Search of Excellence argued that Japanese managers had achieved something remarkable. The Japanese, Peters and Waterman observed, had produced a competitive economy from the rubble of a society that we would do well to remember had, only thirty years previously, been the victim of nuclear attack. Twice!

Yet despite the often-voiced suggestion of that time – that Americans could choose either to work *like* the Japanese or *for* the Japanese – *In Search of Excellence* insisted that there remained, within American management, real pockets of excellence. Thus Peters and Waterman argued that rather than seeking simply to emulate the practices of their Japanese counterparts, American managers could learn from their home-grown contemporaries and in so doing could develop a form of executive leadership that built upon the lessons available from America's best run companies.

The text prepared by Pascale and Athos offered the careful reader a similar account of America's problems and suggested a broadly similar solution. However, the title of this work and its focus upon what was truly good about Japanese management encouraged more casual

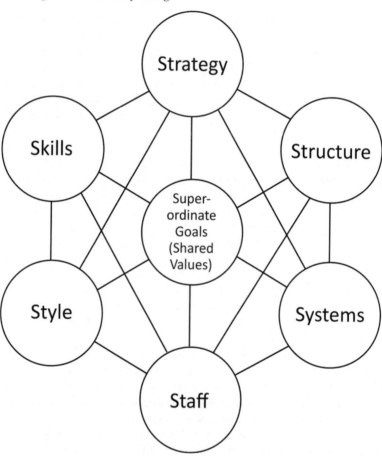

Figure 3.1 McKinsey 7-S model

readers to form the opinion that *The Art of Japanese Management* simply vaunted Japan at America's expense.

In the mid-1980s I obtained my hardback copy of *The Art of Japanese Management* from a 'remaindered' book shop in Glasgow's city centre. And as I recall I paid the princely sum of 50 pence. At the same time *In Search of Excellence* was dominating the bestseller lists; in fact it outsold every other text published in this period, apart from a new edition of the Bible (Collins 2007).

The relative performance of these books is, I believe, instructive for our analysis of organizational storytelling. Despite the obvious symmetry of their texts, therefore, the 'success' of Peters and Waterman and the 'failure' of Pascale and Athos should remind us that if you plan to 'make America great again' you must be careful to construct a narrative that taps into the hopes, aspirations and expectations of your fellow countrymen and women. Get this wrong – offend or disappoint your audience – and your narrative will surely fail to make the emotional connections that will get things done!

Mindful of the need to connect with the expectations of their audience, Peters and Waterman argued that what had made America great in the 1950s – its hard-S capabilities – had made it relatively weak in the 1970s because consumer preferences had altered to demand both quality and innovation (which Japan had delivered in spades!). In an attempt to prepare America for the 1980s and beyond, Peters and Waterman advocated what amounted to a cultural revolution in management (see Wright 1994). Thus the authors argued that, far from pursuing a Taylorised separation of worker and managerial responsibilities, corporate leaders would need to learn how to use the narrative and symbolic tools at their disposal to 'de-separate' the organization. Or, less cryptically, the authors argued that managers would need to develop cultures dedicated to customers, quality and innovation. Outlining the nature of the tools which would deliver such cultures, Peters and Waterman (1982) and later Peters and Austin (1985) argued that managers would need to seek out and should, where necessary, create opportunities to model the forms of thinking and action that would be needed to deliver quality and innovation for customers. Indeed, Peters and his collaborators suggested that managers should take steps – literally – to establish themselves as a visible presence throughout the organization, an approach that soon became known as MBWA, or management by wandering around. In short, Peters (if you will indulge me) recognised that not all who wander are lost. Thus he suggested that in their organizational travels, leaders would need to learn how to exploit the culturally symbolic aspects of employment. Adding welcome detail to this emerging manifesto, Peters advised managers to develop and to cultivate stories which would create models for thinking and feeling and, *beyond this*, exemplars for action in contexts otherwise dominated by division and ambiguity.

The Nobel laureate, John Steinbeck, offers a very useful and, for me, a very moving endorsement of this general position. Thus Steinbeck illustrates the manner in which storytelling and shared talk, more generally, can be used to generate a sense of common purpose.

In his short novel *Of Mice and Men*, Steinbeck ([1937] 1974) constructs an unlikely and ill-starred friendship between two ranch-hands: Lennie, a small and quick-witted man, and George, who remains to all intents and purposes a child in a giant's body. The extract reproduced below is, I believe, useful for our reflections on the ways and means of organizational storytelling for two reasons. First it demonstrates the manner in which stories can act to define our sense of self and our relationships with others. Thus it is worth observing that the tale which George and Lennie share demonstrates the difference between their partnership; their mutual endeavour and the lonely aimlessness of those who are, for the want of a dream made real by a shared story, doomed to spend the rest of their lives moving from place to place and working for others. Second, Steinbeck's text shows clearly the important roles of shared performance and repetition.

George, as we shall soon see, knows very well the story that he will demand to have performed. And yet he *needs* to have Lennie recite the tale. George, of course, pleads that he retains this desire because he tends to omit key parts of the narrative, and so fails to do justice to the tale. But these pleadings are false. Indeed the extract reproduced below gives us every reason to believe that George knows the story well and could render it fully. For me the truth of the matter is that George wants Lennie to tell their shared story because, leaving aside the thrill and enjoyment of a tale well told, he recognises that the narrative acts like a contract, and in getting Lennie to repeat the tale George can be confident that the covenant which forms their plan for a future hereafter still holds.

Steinbeck works hard, I have always thought, to ensure that we understand the significance of this tale and the manner in which it acts to solemnise a doomed undertaking between these unlikely friends. Thus as Lennie relents and begins to tell the tale, Steinbeck takes care to demonstrate that this story has significance precisely because it is so often repeated. As Lennie opens the tale for George and for us, therefore, Steinbeck tells us that his voice changes: It becomes deeper and the words flow rhythmically in a prayer-like fashion. In fact it would not be a stretch to suggest that this shared story is a form of communion.

Our extract, of course, has a context. Every tale we announce is, if we are honest, in the middle of something else! It is important to point out, therefore, that in the moments before our extract commences Lennie has been scolding George. Indeed, the first time that we encounter this unlikely pairing Lennie is castigating his friend because he has been drinking from a stagnant pool.

George, it soon becomes clear, is always getting into some sort of trouble. And what is worse, Lennie, as the grown-up member of the partnership, has to resolve these difficult problems as they arise. So even as the novella begins Lennie is already working on a plan to address the problems that generally develop when poor George is at large in the world of men.

Yet while George is innocent and alarmingly naïve, he is not entirely guileless. He offers no defence when Lennie scolds him for drinking from the pool, nor for all the other difficulties that he has visited upon the partnership. Indeed, George accepts his culpability for the situation and volunteers to resolve both the immediate issue and Lennie's ongoing difficulties by going to live alone, like a hermit, in a cave. Despite the fact that, when criticised, George routinely threatens to adopt the life of a hermit, Lennie quickly relents. Sensing a small personal advantage in this retreat George seizes his opportunity and demands that Lennie recounts the story that defines and brings purpose to their deep and enduring friendship:

Lennie pleaded: 'Come on, George. Tell me. Please, George. Like you done before.'

'You get a kick outta that, don't you. A'right, I'll tell you, and then we'll eat our supper ...'

George's voice became deeper. He repeated his words rhythmically as though he had said them many times before. 'Guys like us, that work on ranches, are the loneliest guys in the world. They got no family. They don't belong no place. They come to a range an' work up a stake and then they go inta town and blow their stake, and the first thing you know they're poundin' their tail on some other ranch. They ain't got nothing to look ahead to.'

Lennie was delighted. 'That's it – that's it. Now tell how it is with us.'

George went on. 'With us it ain't like that. We got a future. We got somebody to talk to that gives a damn about us. We don't have to sit in no bar-room blowin' in our jack jus' because we got no place else to go. If them other guys gets in jail they can rot for all anybody gives a damn. But not us.'

Lennie broke in. '*But not us! An' why? Because ... because I got you to look after me, an you got me to look after you, and that's why.*' He laughed delightedly. 'Go on now, George.'

'You got it by heart. You can do it yourself.'

'No, you. I forget some a' the things. Tell about how it's gonna be.'

'O.K. Some day – we're gonna get the jack together and we're gonna have a little house and a couple of acres an' a cow and some pigs and ...'

'*An' live off the fatta the lan',*' Lennie shouted. 'An' have *rabbits*. Go on, George! Tell about what we're gonna have in the garden

and about the rabbits in the cages and about the rain in the winter
and the stove, and how thick the cream is on the milk like you can
hardly cut it. Tell about that George.'
    'Why'n't you do it yourself. You know all of it.'
    'No ... you tell it. It ain't the same if I tell it. Go on ... George.
How I get to tend the rabbits.'
    'Well,' said George. 'We'll have a big vegetable patch and a
rabbit-hutch and chickens. And when it rains in the winter, we'll
just say the hell with goin' to work.'
                    (Steinbeck [1937] 1974: 17–18, original emphasis).

Most managerial commentators, I suspect, would accept that stories
such as that cherished by George can help individuals to forge the
emotional bonds; the common understanding, and the spirit of co-
operation that *gets things done*. But we should not confuse a superficial
agreement on these matters with a deep and abiding consensus. Indeed
we must be clear that the academic field concerned with organizational
storytelling is scarred by debates which, while they are often over-
looked in the texts that have been prepared for practitioners of management, nonetheless actively contest both the nature of stories and the
organizing capability of these narratives. We may begin to explore this
under-explored terrain through a comparison of 'sensemaking' and
'sensegiving' perspectives on organizational storytelling.

Sensemaking and sensegiving perspectives

Sensemaking accounts of organizational storytelling tend to draw their
inspiration from the work of Karl Weick (1993; 1995). Weick has become
a leading figure in the study of management and organization, in part,
because he offers a distinctive account of the dynamics of managerial
work which places narrative at the very centre of organizational life.
    Challenging the subject–object divide at the heart of social theory
(see Cunliffe 2011), Weick argues that, on a day-to-day basis, each of
us is obliged to navigate our lives under conditions that are marked by
complexity and ambiguity. To reduce the complexity and to filter the
ambiguity that threatens to engulf us, Weick suggests that we are
obliged to construct personal narratives that situate and explain our
problems; our emotions and our ambitions. Furthermore he suggests
that – having constructed these narratives – we then tend to navigate
our lives *as if* these constructs represent neutral, dispassionate, observations of an external reality. For Weick, therefore, social life and
social action are, despite appearances to the contrary, constructed in

and through narratives. What gets done, he suggests, is whatever has a good story.

And what makes for a good story? Weick suggest that good stories, narratives that animate and orientate, are, while grounded in reality, driven by plausibility rather than by accuracy.

In an attempt to situate and to explain what is actually a rather challenging conceptualisation of identity and organization, Weick (1995) considers the social construction of 'battered child syndrome'. Through this analysis Weick is able to demonstrate the essential distinction between 'interpretation' and 'enactment' and the role which storytelling performs in the constitution of sensible environments.

Battered child syndrome

Thanks to a number of high-profile and, frankly, appalling court cases which have examined allegations of child neglect and physical harm, the idea that children might be assaulted or even killed by those who have been entrusted with their care is now all too familiar. Weick (1995) however, reminds us that 'battered child syndrome' is actually a very recent medical phenomenon. Of course Weick does not suggest that at some point in our history we enjoyed an idealised era when children and young people received only love and care from those who exercised routine power over their lives; there are just too many recorded instances of assault and abuse to sustain such an assertion (see Cockburn 1991). Weick is, however, keen to trace the processes of narrative formation and identity construction which make 'battered child syndrome' a sensible explanation of events that have not been witnessed directly.

So why do we now have a medical diagnosis that recognises the systematic abuse of children within familial contexts and within other training and/or care establishments? Or, putting this another way: why was 'battered child syndrome' once unthinkable amongst medical practitioners?

The short answer is that 'battered child syndrome' remained literally unthinkable for so long as alternative, plausible explanations for the injuries reported by children were allowed to endure. Pursuing the processes which sustained the pretence that children would not be assaulted by the adults charged with their care, Weick suggests that medical doctors were inclined to accept, or perhaps more truthfully, were inclined to co-construct, case histories for childhood injuries refracted through the lens of their own childhood experiences. Thus Weick suggests that, having come from homes that were for the most part stable and nurturing, clinicians were inclined to co-construct narratives which insisted that the young people who had been brought to their surgeries had been harmed through accidental events. These children were assumed to be loved but reckless. They were cared for but clumsy. Thus a combination of (a) deceitful parents or carers who were prepared to offer false case histories, and (b) medical practitioners willing to cultivate narratives that sought congruence with their own identities, rendered systematic child abuse more or less unfathomable.

Through his analysis of 'battered child syndrome' Weick reminds us that we do not simply 'interpret' events. Rather, we 'enact' events within environments shaped by our own identities. In this respect 'battered child syndrome' was rendered unthinkable in so many emergency rooms because it conflicted with the ideas, orientations and experiences of clinicians. Yet Weick is also keen to point out that beyond this elite, others within the medical establishment – radiographic technicians who were subordinate to and altogether less privileged than the clinicians – were inclined to enact alternative sensible environments that made 'assault' a plausible diagnosis.

Radiographic materials – X-ray photographs – are important in the enactment of these newly abusive environments for they allowed the radiographers to challenge the case histories constructed by the clinicians. Thus Weick suggests that radiographers were able to observe the primary complaint that had brought the child to the doctor, say a fractured arm, *and* perhaps just visible on the edge of the photographic plate, older injuries that had partially healed – say fractured ribs. Observing that these secondary injuries had not been reported and had therefore remained untreated, the radiographers were able to challenge the established pattern of sensemaking (the child is clumsy but cared for) and, perhaps more importantly were able to suggest the presence of alternative and abusive relationships. For if the parents in the waiting room were truly the loving guardians of a clumsy or reckless child how could they have failed to notice cracked ribs? Why, for example, would the loving parents developed in and through the clinicians' narrative fail to seek treatment for the sort of incident that could cause fractured ribs? Indeed, if the parents were truly caring and loving, why would they have failed to report the weeks of obvious pain and discomfort that is experienced while cracked ribs heal?

Sensegiving accounts of organizational storytelling (see Gioia and Chittipeddi 1991) build upon and yet modify Weick's analysis of sensemaking. Thus sensegiving accounts of storytelling suggest that *since* all of us are obliged to construct and navigate our lives narratively and *since* action in organizations stems from such narrative constructions, managers *should* intervene in organizational processes, and in order to craft and deploy stories designed to enact their preferred goals. The problem being, as we shall see, that sensegiving accounts of storytelling tend to presume that managers can, fairly readily, produce purpose and direction for their employees.

Esler (2012) captures this sensegiving approach rather well. However, he acknowledges the very real efforts required to sustain stories in contexts shaped by politically laden ambiguities.

As an experienced journalist and broadcaster, Esler plainly knows a thing or two about storytelling and is, it seems, now keen to share what he has learned with those who have been entrusted with the management of our corporations. Perhaps unsurprisingly Esler suggests that managers can *make things happen* through storytelling. But he is keen to point out that this outcome will materialise only so long as the tales, crafted and rendered, have been designed to colonize the consciousness of the audience:

> The secret weapon of storytellers throughout the centuries has been to create a story which sticks in the mind, just as a successful musician will write a pop song with a melody so powerful that you cannot get it out of your head. Germans call this an *Ohrwurm*, literally an 'earworm', or 'earwig', which won't stop wriggling whether you like it or not, until it worms its way into your brain. Successful leaders work hard at creating an 'earwig', or they employ others to do it for them. They spend a lot of time wondering how to communicate their leadership story and subvert the counter-stories told against them.
>
> (Esler 2012: 19, original emphasis)

Denning (2001) offers a concrete illustration of Esler's argument: In *The Springboard*, Denning, then, a senior employee of the World Bank, confesses that he had tried and failed to convince his colleagues of the virtues of a key infrastructure project designed to bring clean water to the villages and homes of those living in the developing world. Denning confesses that nothing – not charts, nor reports, nor statistical analyses – would move his colleagues until, he tells us, he happened upon a tale, which in grim but deeply human terms, illustrated the effort that women and small children in parts of Africa have to exert daily in order to collect and to carry water. This story, Denning tells us, acted as 'a springboard' since it demonstrated to the audience present that very small children are, too often, denied the opportunity of an elementary education because they are obliged to spend most of each and every day collecting what we allow to drip wastefully from our taps.

Reflecting upon this performance, Denning argues that his story acted as a 'springboard', an emotional lever for action because it demonstrated to those who remained unmoved by logical argument and rational calculation that something *should* be done. And perhaps more importantly it showed that something *could* be done to resolve this dreadful situation. Thus Denning's 'springboard story' *caused and allowed* change because it removed those obstacles that had prevented colleagues from supporting the infrastructure programme that Denning knew to be vital.

The former British prime minister Gordon Brown (2010) offers similar testimony as to the power of organizational storytelling, and in so doing shows a command of rhetorical poetics which few suspected. Recounting his efforts to ensure that the developed world would honour its 'millennium' funding commitments to Africa, Brown recalls addressing a meeting of forty-five leaders whom, he feared, were starting to draw back from their undertakings. In an attempt to prevent this withdrawal of funding Brown tells us that he relayed what we will term 'the story of David'.

David, Brown tells us, was a child who had the misfortune to be born in Rwanda during a particularly turbulent period of its history. Discussing David's short life, Brown reveals that this poor child (and indeed many, many more like him) was murdered in the Rwandan genocide, a terrible, brutal, vicious, pre-industrial form of 'ethnic cleansing' (Gourevitch 1998). Standing before the leaders of the richest and most powerful nations in the world, Brown tells us that he used the story of the child David to educate his audience about what happens when those who could act choose not to fulfil their moral obligations. Confronting his contemporaries with the brutal facts of David's death, therefore, Brown told the representatives of the other forty-four nations who were, he feared, looking for opportunities to wriggle out of their funding commitments, that a photograph of this young boy now hangs in a memorial hall in Kigali (the capital of Rwanda). Beneath the picture, those who can bear to look may read:

His name:	David
His age:	10
His favourite sport:	football
His passion in life:	making people laugh
His dream:	to become a medical doctor
His cause of death:	tortured to death
His last words on earth:	'The UN will come for us.'

This list and Brown's account of 'David' constitutes a narrative product. And perhaps more importantly this is a story that actually made something happen: It helped to ensure that the world's leaders would honour their funding commitments to Africa.

Taken together, Esler's 'earworms', Denning's 'springboard stories' and Brown's 'story of David' demonstrate that poetic tales have a capacity (a) to tap emotions, (b) to shape understanding, and (c) to precipitate action. Indeed, it is worth observing that Brown's story and Denning's 'springboard' *do things* because they plant and propagate narratives which humanise events, and in so doing make real problems which had hitherto appeared to be merely abstract, or somehow far-removed from other more pressing or more local concerns. Yet we should not assume that all those who would endorse a 'sensegiving' account of storytelling actually agree on what stories can do within the workplace.

Tom Peters (see Peters and Waterman 1982; Peters and Austin 1985) places storytelling at the very core of managerial work. Indeed, for Peters, storytelling is essentially synonymous with managing. Those who would get things done, Peters insists, need to craft and share narratives that will allow others to understand that what needs to be done is, in truth, useful and worthy. Denning accepts much of this argument. Yet he seems to suggest that stories perform an ancillary organizational function, and so exercise their effects only at key junctures. Thus where Peters suggests that 'talk' is what managers (should) do all day and every day, Denning seems to insist upon a separation between 'talk' and 'action'. For Denning, therefore, springboard tales are useful as projects commence or stall because they can help to engender a common sense of purpose. But springboard stories, Denning insists, will not dig wells. At some point, he argues, the talking needs to stop and the digging needs to start. Peters, however, would find it difficult to accept this. Indeed he would counter that Denning's attempt to separate 'talk' and 'action' is wrong at a conceptual level and wrong-headed at a practical level, not least because managers need to sustain and, periodically, will need to repair and/or renew the moral projects that they are obliged to construct in and through stories. And for once I am inclined to agree with Peters (for an account of the more typical disagreements that shape my relationship with Tom Peters see Collins (1998; 2000; 2007)). But we must move on. This little book is not about Tom Peters, nor is it in any sense devoted to Denning. It is about the nature of stories and the craft of storytelling, and it is time we considered the divisions that persist *within* sensemaking accounts of organizational storytelling.

Divisions within sensemaking accounts

Sensegiving accounts of organizational storytelling generally concede that it can be a challenge to make sense for others through stories. Indeed you will recall that Esler (2012) suggests that managers may have to take steps to subvert the narratives developed by, say, competitors, managerial rivals or trades union officials. Nonetheless advocates of 'sensegiving' generally assert that managerial leaders – when appropriately trained and supported – may use stories, reliably, to control the thoughts and actions of others. In contrast, sensemaking perspectives on storytelling tend to view stories as natural resources; spontaneous elements of social life which well up, as you might expect, from the bottom of organizations. In broad terms, therefore, the sensemaking account of organizational storytelling suggests that the stories which we tell ourselves, and others, offer important insights into the complexities of management and the essential plurality of social organization. Where sensegiving perspectives portray stories as managerial tools that may be deployed to control others, therefore, sensemaking perspectives counter that stories provide employees with a focus for dissent and a basis for resistance (Boje 1991; 2001; Gabriel 1995; 1998; 2000).

Gabriel (2000) has been especially keen to explore and to reveal the subversive potential of organizational storytelling. His analysis begins by observing that discontent with modernist scholarship has redeemed the 'story' from its position as a quaint subordinate to the facts of 'history' such that stories are now widely acknowledged to be not merely reflections of organizational life, but creators of organizational meaning and organizational realities.

Gabriel observes that contemporary academic interest in storytelling has been facilitated by postmodern scholarship and its tendency to see stories (as generators and creators of meaning) everywhere. Yet Gabriel disputes this tendency to 'see stories everywhere' – as the creators and generators of meaning – on two counts. First, as we shall see below, he argues that not all narratives qualify as stories. Second, he insists that stories do not always and everywhere generate and sustain meaning, because while stories are portable they are often modified as they travel. Thus Gabriel suggests that stories have a fragile and 'polysemic' quality, which makes them susceptible to translation (Latour 1987).

Boje's (1991; 2001) analysis of narratives and 'narratology' demonstrates a similar concern with polysemy. Reflecting upon the corporate successes and excesses of the Nike corporation, for example, Boje et al. (2001) argue that the stories of the oppressed (who produce Nike apparel) may help to break down the fantasies (Gabriel 1995; 2000;

2004), which have grown up around the consumption of Nike. Contrasting the stories which Nike likes to tell about its policies and endeavours in the Third World (Nike as the handmaiden of economic development and social improvement), with the tales which Nike's employees in these lesser developed countries tell of their experiences (Nike as violent corporate predator), Boje et al. (2001) have sought to 're-story' Nike, in the hope of generating an alternative understanding of the life and work of this corporation. Comparing Nike's official history with grass-roots stories which reflect more fully the experiences of employees who work for Nike in the Third World, Boje argues that his 're-storying' endeavours make it difficult for this corporation to produce and sustain the carefully crafted tales of corporate benevolence which it has been keen to share with the general public.

Writing alone, Boje (2001) has subsequently developed a more challenging account of organizational storytelling which attempts to tease out the deeper implications of his 're-storying' endeavours. Following Weick's (1995) account of sensemaking, Boje observes that, on a day-to-day basis, people confront a key problem: how to make sense of a 'complex soup' of ambiguous and half-understood problems, events and experiences. Reflecting upon this problem of ambiguity, Boje suggests that people construct and retrace their lives, retrospectively, through stories. For Boje (2001), therefore, stories have a particular significance and a distinctive meaning. Indeed Boje warns us that we must distinguish 'stories' from 'narratives' if we are to understand the richness of organizational sensemaking. Thus Boje argues that 'narratives' are not to be confused with stories. Narratives, he argues, stand aloof from the flow of experience. Narratives are, he warns, plotted, directed and staged to produce a linear, coherent and monological rendering of events, while 'stories are self-deconstructing, flowing, emerging and networking, not at all static' (Boje 2001: 1).

Commenting upon the narrative understanding of organization, which comes to us from such august sources as the *Harvard Business Review* (see also Collins and Rainwater 2005), Boje argues that academic analysis has, too often, confused stories with more linear and monological narrative forms. Indeed he complains that 'so much of what passes for academic narrative analysis in organization studies seems to rely upon sequential, single-voiced stories' (Boje 2001: 9). In an attempt to provide an alternative to these monologues of business endeavour, Boje introduces the concept of the 'antenarrative', which, he argues, resituates the concerns of the field of organizational storytelling – directing inquiry towards a concern with flux and emergence.

This focus upon flow and fragmentation has a profound affect on Boje's antenarrative conceptualisation of stories.

Antenarratives and terse tales

For Boje (2001), 'antenarrative' has two faces. On one face, Boje's focus upon 'antenarrative' is based upon the assertion that 'stories' precede 'narrative'. Thus Boje suggests that stories are 'antenarrative' insofar as they come before the processes of staging and directing, which, as he sees it, lead to the development of 'sequential, single-voiced', top-down 'narratives'. On the obverse face, Boje calls upon the rules of poker and suggests that an 'antenarrative' represents 'a bet' (or 'an ante') that retrospective sensemaking may emerge in the future from 'the fragmented, non-linear, incoherent, collective and unplotted' (1) stories, which come before corporate monologues.

This account of stories and narratives overlaps to some degree with the account offered by Gabriel (2000). In common with Boje, Gabriel observes that stories offer local and intimate accounts of situations, events and predicaments. Indeed, reflecting upon the complexities associated with the analysis of stories and storytelling, Gabriel argues that storywork – literally the art of constructing meaningful stories – is a delicately woven product of intimate knowledge.

At one level of analysis Gabriel (1998; 2000) seems to agree with Boje that a story represents a speculative bet on the shape of the future. Indeed he tells us that when a storyteller announces a tale – and so seeks the temporary suspension of the normal rules of conversational exchange – s/he forms a covenant with the audience which promises to trade amusement/enlightenment/edification for a prolonged, if temporary, and attentive silence. Furthermore, Gabriel concurs with Boje that it is vitally important to distinguish 'stories' from other 'narrative' forms. Yet at this point the accounts of storytelling prepared by Boje and Gabriel diverge quite fundamentally.

Commenting upon the craft of storytelling, both Boje and Gabriel have complained that nowadays it can be difficult to unearth good stories and talented storytellers in organizations. Indeed, each has suggested that it is becoming increasingly difficult to witness organizational storytelling in its naturally intimate surroundings. Pondering the cause of this narrative deskilling, both authors suggest that contemporary developments which have acted to intensify the pace of working life reduce the opportunity for spontaneous interaction at work and thus diminish the opportunities available to craft and to share stories (see also Bunting 2005). This shared recognition of poetic decline, however, takes Boje and Gabriel in opposite analytical directions. Lamenting the perceived decline in organizational stories, Gabriel (2000) simply renews his commitment to the understanding that stories are (increasingly rare and) special forms of narrative with definite characteristics. Boje, however, adopts a rather different approach which seeks to redefine the very nature of organizational stories. In an initial move, Boje (1991) suggests that the four words which announce: 'you know the story' constitute a poetic tale. Later in a more radical move Boje (2001) suggests, as we have seen, that stories should be regarded as those special forms of narrative that exist *prior* to the crystallising processes of casting and plotting.

Gabriel, however, disputes these moves and I tend to agree with his reasoning (see Collins 2007). For Gabriel, stories – despite literary deskilling – represent a rich and, in any sense, a vital resource for organizational theorists. And on this matter he and Boje are in perfect agreement: stories are interesting because they allow us to experience the dynamic flow that is social organization. But for Gabriel plots, staging and direction need to be recognised as constituting the central characteristics of stories. Taking issue with Boje's first move, therefore, Gabriel protests that while the, so-called, 'terse stories' observed by Boje represent invitations to recall either a pattern of events or a particular rendering of a tale, they are not, properly-speaking, stories. Thus Gabriel warns us that Boje's attempt to frame the art of storytelling within the four words which offer the reassurance that 'you know the story' lacks 'performativity, memorableness, ingenuity and symbolism' (Gabriel 2000: 20). In an attempt to illustrate this rather important point we will pause to consider the very short story attributed to the author Ernest Hemingway.

Hemingway, it has been suggested, was of the opinion that a short story could be completed in just a handful of words and offered the following example: *Baby shoes for sale, not worn*. These words, I believe, operate reasonably well as a notice advertising goods for sale. In addition I will readily concede that these six words might provide the inspiration necessary to develop a useful story. Yet this phrase does not in itself constitute a tale. Indeed, if Hemingway's six words do amount to a story, we might reasonably ask: 'what kind of story is this?'

Is Hemingway's terse story a sad tale? Was the baby for whom the shoes were intended stillborn?

Or is this a lighter tale? Is there perhaps a funny story located within the embryo of these six words that explains why these shoes remain 'as new'?

Personally I could envisage any number of quite different tales built upon the inspiration of these six words. And that surely is the problem! For if we tell stories in organized settings to orientate ourselves (and the others around us) then it should be apparent that Hemingway's six-word story fails because, far from providing the narrative materials that will enact sensible environments, this so-called tale simply abrogates this responsibility! It says construct your own sensible environment. Tell yourself any tale you like!

Similar problems persist with Boje's 'terse tale'. Thus to suggest that the invocation 'you know the story' is, in any sense, equivalent to arranging actors and events within a plotted environment, is surely to misunderstand both the nature of stories and their enduring appeal.

It is, I grant you, fairly clear that an utterance designed to reassure another person that they are already familiar with a story might encourage this individual to recall a series of events. Yet this is not the same as telling as story because, on their own, these four words carry with them no reassurance that the person who has been asked to use their powers of recollection will build a world that is, in any sense, congruent with the needs and orientations of the person who first voiced the suggestion that each of those present holds a common perspective and understanding. Thus Boje's 'terse tale' fails what we might call 'the George and Lennie test' because it so plainly lacks the capacity to construct a world within which common dreams might be built and pursued. Similar concerns, as we shall see, apply to Boje's (2001) antenarrative conceptualisation of organizational stories.

Boje's suspicion of narrative monologues, as we have seen, stems from a concern that academics and business commentators have been, altogether, too keen to endorse a sensegiving account of storytelling and have, as a consequence colonised the organizational world with tales that are linear, single-voiced and top-down in their orientation. Noting both, the practical consequences and the analytical limitations of such sensegiving accounts of storytelling, Boje (2001) suggest that we should be suspicious of corporate plotting and should, in an attempt to free ourselves from such hegemonies, embrace antenarratives which as the name suggests come before the crystallising processes of plot formation. This antenarrative approach to storytelling has become pretty popular, and a number of authors (see for example Adorisio 2009) have attempted to apply its key tenets to a range of contemporary issues and settings. And yet I find this antenarrative conceptualization unhelpful and broadly unconvincing. I do recognise, of course, that the antenarrative concept usefully directs our attention to the contested sensemaking processes that circulate as organizational members attempt to come to terms with novel events. Furthermore, I accept that as organizational members begin to narrate novel events there may be a period when the meaning(s) and/or the significance of such movements and moments remains volatile and subject to sudden plot changes. But I find it difficult to accept the utility of a narrative that, as Boje suggests, escapes or otherwise seeks to evade the strictures of plot, place and time. Indeed I find it difficult to discern the difference between an antenarrative and a bad story that simply breaches the covenant formed between speaker and audience! I suggest, therefore, that what Boje terms an antenarrative story might more usefully be regarded as being – at best – a 'proto-story'. To elaborate on this point, Chapter 4 will consider a number of alternative, if related, narrative forms, namely the 'reports', 'opinions', 'proto-stories' and 'poetic stories' outlined by Gabriel (2000).

4   Reports, opinions and proto-stories

In this chapter we will consider narrative types. We will commence by reviewing the differences between 'stories' and 'reports' and we will conclude by examining the ways in which storytellers may rearrange characters and events to produce a pleasing effect. Yet having initially indulged a categorical distinction between stories and reports, we will attempt to demonstrate that reports – even those which make the most stubborn protestations as to their factuality – build and depend upon the tools of the storyteller. Having challenged this general division between 'stories' and 'reports', we will then offer more detailed reflections on narratives and narrative forms. Thus we will examine 'deductive' and 'inductive' accounts of storytelling as we attempt to clarify the essential nature of the poetic tale. So that you might apply this now more nuanced appreciation of the structural characteristics of the poetic tale to the problems and processes of managerial work, we will conclude by offering a pro forma designed to allow you to reflect upon the narrative components that will be required to build and to sustain 'epic', 'comic', 'romantic' and 'tragic' tales within your workplace.

* * *

Box 4.1 A report

At 2:43, early in the morning of 21 May, a 999 call was placed with the Emergency Services. The caller requested the Fire Service. The BT operator – as is normal practice – confirmed the telephone number of the caller and transferred the request to the Northwich Fire Service Control Room. The man on the other end of the line identified himself as one David Collins of Waxham Road, Northwich.

Calmly and very deliberately he stated that number 497 Waxham Road was on fire. He commented that the building was well alight and pointed out – again very deliberately – that the property was the subject of ongoing building work and had been unoccupied for some time.

Two tenders from Northwich Fire and Rescue Service were on the scene within 5 minutes. Arriving at the address, the fire crews encountered a number of local police officers. As a precaution these officers had already closed the road to foot and vehicular traffic.

The fire was quickly brought under control and was, effectively, extinguished within one hour. Fire Service personnel remained in attendance, however, to damp down the embers and to guard against re-ignition, until 7 a.m.

An opinion

The fire across the way? No, I slept through the whole thing.

What I did hear, though, is that the police suspect arson.

Her along the road – at 515 – told me as much. She heard that the owner started the fire himself. But I don't go for that. *I* spoke to his wife.

No if you ask me he's the victim in all this because I think the fire was pay-back.

You look puzzled. Did you not know?

He happens to be a former night-club owner with some shady associates. And if you ask me this whole incident smacks of the underworld.

Noting the importance of plotting and performance in the art of storytelling, Gabriel (2000) has attempted to forge a categorical distinction between organizational stories and the other, related, narrative forms commonly found in organized settings (see the boxed text for an illustration of the ways in which these different narrative forms may seek to account for events). Thus Gabriel argues that there is a need to distinguish:

- **'Reports'**

Reports, Gabriel argues, offer an historic rather than a poetic rendering of events. Reports, therefore, produce stubbornly factual and causative, as opposed to symbolic, accounts. Reports, Gabriel adds, are monological. They invite factual verification, and so, seek to crystallise our understanding of events.

• 'Opinions'

Opinions are similar to stories insofar as both may contain factual and symbolic materials. However Gabriel's analysis suggests that these 'opinions' seek to 'tell' rather than to 'show' the audience what has happened. Consequently 'opinions' may lack the seductive qualities necessary to convince others that the events under scrutiny are fully relevant to their concerns or, somehow, consonant with their experience.

Box 4.2 A proto-story

Yes – the report from the fire control room is accurate. In other circumstances I might not have remembered the date but May 21st is my younger son – Daniel's – birthday and I recall the events of May 20th/21st rather well.

May 20th had been one of those lovely, early summer days – warm without being oppressive. My wife and I had been up late on that evening getting things ready for Daniel's birthday.

I had already blown up enough balloons to make me feel rather giddy when Katy – that's my wife – announced that we would have to wrap Daniel's new scooter. I had suggested that we should, simply, attach a ribbon to the handlebars but had been over-ruled. So at 10:30 we had begun wrapping the scooter. This job took just about as long as one might expect, and so, we retired rather later than normal.

At some point in the night; around half-past-two – I think – I was woken by my wife. She announced, rather sharply, that it was raining heavily and that we would need to close some of the larger windows that we had left open to cool the house. But as she approached the first window she received a shock. She discovered that the noise she had taken to be rain was, in fact, the sound of burning embers falling on and around our house. She beckoned me to the window calling, 'Come and see this; the house across the road is on fire!'

I responded to her instruction but paused to collect the telephone *en route*. Confirming the fact of the fire I promptly dialled 999 and asked for the Fire Brigade. When I was connected I informed the operator that 497 Waxham Road was on fire. Actually this was incorrect. In fact it was the house at 495 which was alight. But the Fire Brigade aren't so fussy about such things. If it's alight they'll put it out.

> But I did get one rather important detail correct. Recalling a story my own mother had told me when I was just 7 years old I informed the operator that the property was – to the best of my knowledge – unoccupied at night.

• 'Proto-stories'

Classical formulations of the poetic tale (see Aristotle 1965) suggest that stories develop an interaction between scene, actor and plot that proceeds to a satisfactory conclusion. Gabriel's 'proto-stories' contain some but not all of these elements. They are therefore prototypical insofar as future rehearsal and/or embellishment may create those missing elements that make this narrative form unsatisfactory. Thus 'proto-stories', like Boje's antenarratives, may have some level of characterisation but will remain incomplete and broadly unsatisfactory because, for example, they lack a plot that can deliver a useful ending.

• 'Poetic tales'

Poetic tales, or if you prefer, *proper* stories, are local, organic and polyphonic in character. Furthermore they depend upon embellishment and the exercise of poetic licence for the generation of meaning. Charles Dickens understands this and communicates his appreciation rather well. Indeed he takes special care to warn his readers that the success of *A Christmas Carol* will depend upon their commitment to, and their collusion in, the exercise of poetic licence. Thus Dickens begins his classic tale with the following observations:

> Marley was dead: to begin with. There is no doubt whatever about that. The register of his burial was signed by the clergyman, the clerk, the undertaker, and the chief mourner. Scrooge signed it: and Scrooge's name was good upon 'Change, for anything he chose to put his hand to. Old Marley was dead as a door-nail.
>
> Mind! I don't mean to say that I know, of my own knowledge, what there is particularly dead about a door-nail. I might have been inclined, myself, to regard a coffin-nail as the deadest piece of ironmongery in the trade. But the wisdom of our ancestors is in the similie; and my unhallowed hands shall not disturb it, or the Country's done for. You will therefore permit me to repeat, emphatically, that Marley was dead as a door-nail.
>
> Scrooge knew he was dead? Of course he did. How could it be otherwise? Scrooge and he were partners for I don't know how

many years. Scrooge was his sole executor, his sole administrator, his sole assign, his sole residuary legatee, his sole friend and sole mourner. And even Scrooge was not so dreadfully cut up by the sad event, but that he was an excellent man of business on the very day of the funeral, and solemnised it with an undoubted bargain.

The mention of Marley's funeral brings me back to the point I started from. There is no doubt that Marley was dead. This must be distinctly understood, or nothing wonderful can come of the story I am going to relate. If we were not perfectly convinced that Hamlet's father died before the play began, there would be nothing more remarkable in his taking a stroll at night, in an easterly wind, upon his own ramparts, than there would be in any middle-aged man rashly turning out after dark in a breezy spot – say Saint Paul's Churchyard for instance – literally to astonish his son's weak mind.

(Dickens, [1841] 1922: 1–3)

Elaborating further upon the exercise of this poetic licence Gabriel (2000; 2004) draws our attention to the 6Fs of narrative construction.

Box 4.3 A proper story

The story that my mother told me? Yes of course I should elaborate.

But a few words of prefacing are called for. You see this is an heroic tale. An heroic tale in two senses.

It is heroic, first, because it deals with fire, smoke and with brave deeds. In a larger sense, I suppose, the tale also deals with obligation and with trust among men. But, perhaps more importantly, it is an heroic story because the narrator is not the hero. Indeed the hero of this tale – a man that I remain rather close to – has never once spoken of these events to me.

Who is the hero? He is my brother-in-law and his name is Bill. He married my oldest sister when I was just 3 years old. And I could not have been more pleased for Bill was a fireman and as every boy knows fire-fighters (as we must call them nowadays) along with train drivers, crane operators, soldiers, pilots, sailors, nuclear technicians, footballers, poachers and astronauts are a breed apart.

When I was just 7 years old my mother told me about a 'shout' (that is what fire-fighters call an emergency) that Bill and his watch had been called to attend. A tenement block – unusual in our part of Ayrshire and partially derelict – was on fire. The fire-fighters, however, could not be sure that this tenement building was unoccupied, and so Bill, Stevie and Ian Montgomery (I suppose that there must have been another Ian on the watch since Ian was always 'Ian Montgomery') were instructed to undertake a search of the premises.

Bill, Stevie and 'Ian Montgomery' quickly donned their 'breathing apparatus' and did what most of us choose not to do: they ran into a burning building. What happened next is unclear – but, in truth, the next few minutes are really not important to our tale – suffice to say that three men entered the burning building and some ten minutes later only two emerged.

The building was unoccupied. Or it had been. Now it had a sole occupant for, somehow, Stevie had been left behind. Without a second thought – and choosing to ignore the fact that they would soon approach the limits of their oxygen supply – Bill and 'Ian Montgomery' re-entered the building. Despite the vision of hell that awaited them within the tenement they somehow managed to locate Stevie. He was on the third floor. A burning ceiling had fallen upon him – bringing with it part of a doorway. Stevie was trapped. And his initial efforts to free himself had caused serious burns to his hands.

When Bill and 'Ian Montgomery' found Stevie he was in a semi-conscious state. And for this fact we should probably be grateful because in the intense heat of the fire Stevie's protective clothing had begun to smoulder. I'm not clear what guidance the Fire Service College provides on the rescue of colleagues in these circumstances. So I don't know if Bill played it by the book or simply improvised. What I know is that between them Bill and 'Ian Montgomery' took Stevie by the collar of his now smouldering jacket and dragged him – at a run – from the building. Later at the hospital, doctors discovered that Stevie had suffered burns to his hands and legs, cracked ribs, a mild concussion and bruising to his calves and buttocks – probably as a direct result of being 'walked Spanish' down three flights of stairs.

Within three months Stevie was back on active service. But he had risked his life needlessly for the want of just a few shards of information! That's what my mother taught me and that is why I took care to tell the operator exactly what I knew about the burning house on Waxham Road.

But that's not the only tale I have concerning Stevie ... The last time I saw Stevie – words which would normally introduce a tragic tale – was in Kilmarnock Infirmary. I was around 10 years old at the time and I had travelled to the hospital with my father to visit one of his friends.

In those days I would fasten myself to just about any opportunity that presented itself to step out with my father. But I had a particular reason for accompanying him that night. You see he was visiting a friend that I happened to like especially. This man had *been* a father. But, tragically, his boy had died when still a child. And, as so often happens, my father's friend had chosen to manage his loss and his grief by becoming a friend to all the children of the world ... or at least to the children of our district. Uniquely in the adult world this was a man who had, always, a kind word for children. And when my dad scolded me for some thoughtlessness or stupidity his friend was always good for a wink that said more plainly than any words ever could – 'It's OK kid.'

I hadn't expected to find Stevie in the hospital that evening. But I was glad that I had. My father's dear old friend was dying and it was plain to me that they had some things that they needed to say to one another. Noting that Stevie had no visitors whatsoever – a fact which surprised me because he had a wife and many friends – I took it upon myself to be his visitor.

Stevie was 'in traction', and so I naturally enquired about the cause of his recent misfortune. He informed me that he had suffered a rather bizarre accident. He had, it seems, paid a visit to a friend. But when he had arrived at this friend's house he discovered that his pal was not at home. However the friend's wife – Mrs MacPherson – had been at home and she had asked Stevie for a favour. Ever the obliging sort Stevie, had gone up to Mrs MacPherson's bedroom to change a light bulb. Unable to reach the socket housed in the ceiling he had climbed on to a dressing table and that is when disaster struck, for the dressing table collapsed, pitching Stevie out of the first floor window.

When my father had concluded his sorry business he collected me from Stevie's bedside. He and Stevie exchanged a few, rather strained, words – or so it seemed to me – and then my father signaled that it was time to leave. I shouted a cheery goodbye to my father's friend and was rewarded with a 'tut' from the matron and a wink (of course) from this very kindly man.

A few minutes later as we walked out of the hospital I recounted Stevie's tale for my father's benefit. Remembering his earlier hospitalisation I also commented on his bad luck. To my surprise my father seemed, already, to know of Stevie's misfortune. Indeed he commented, cryptically, that this fireman was not *so* unlucky as some might imagine. Elaborating on this my father confided that a friend had told him of Stevie's recent hospitalisation. Furthermore my father suggested that aspects of the tale, which Stevie had told me, simply didn't add up. When I asked my father to explain he told me he had heard that when the ambulance found Stevie in the garden he was wearing neither shoes nor trousers. Puzzled by this additional information I asked my father, 'So whatever was Stevie doing in Mrs MacPherson's bedroom?'

My father looked at me and after a lengthy – and slightly uncomfortable – silence he replied, 'I don't know son, but I don't think he was changing light bulbs.'

The '6Fs' of narratives

Gabriel (2000; 2004), as we have seen, argues that stories are unlike 'reports'. Reporters, he suggests, are required to chronicle events whereas stories indulge embellishment. Storytellers, therefore, must be allowed to rearrange characters, situations and events in order to secure the attention and the ongoing affiliation of their audiences. Pursuing this crucial distinction between reportage and storytelling, Gabriel (2004) tells us that poetic tales call upon one or a number of ('6F'), factors. Namely:

Framing
Focusing
Filtering
Fading
Fusing
Fitting

Framing

Stories are not simple assemblies of events nor are they collections of fact. They are artful constructions; careful arrangements of plots and characters. We can gain useful insights in to the processes which (re) arrange characters and events; making these either central or peripheral to the plot by pausing to consider the film *Memphis Belle*.

The film *Memphis Belle* is set in England during the latter stages of World War II when many young men were dispatched from the USA to fly daylight missions against targets in Germany and occupied Europe. Middlebrook and Everett (1985) have extensively documented the Allied air campaign. Writing on his own Middlebrook (1985) also provides a comprehensive account of the attacks which were mounted against Schweinfurt and Regensburg in 1943. In addition he documents the diversionary raids that were organized as attempts to confuse the German ground and air defences. Indeed, it is worth observing that Middlebrook documents the plans which had been carefully developed to swamp these defensive measures. Furthermore he shows the manner in which these plans unravelled due to a combination of poor weather and, frankly, mismanagement.

As Middlebrook's (1985) account of the Schweinfurt raid progresses he sketches, in broad terms, the consequences of these poor manage- ment choices. On a crew-by-crew basis, for example, he is able to track the manner in which a failure to keep to the plan caused young men to die. It is important to note, however, that while Middlebrook is keen to honour the endeavours of the US Eighth Air Force he is no simple warmonger. He is, for example, not at all insensitive to the fate of those on the ground in Schweinfurt and Regensburg on 17 August 1943.

Unlike Middlebrook's (1985) text, the film *Memphis Belle* focuses upon the crew of a single American bomber and its mission to Schwein- furt during the summer of 1943. This frame acts to reconstitute and to reduce the events which Middlebrook so carefully examines.

Perhaps the most obvious difference between these accounts of the Schweinfurt raids relates to the fact that Middlebrook's concern is documentary whereas *Memphis Belle*'s is dramatic. Operating within this dramatised context the film, which is of course based upon actual events, chooses to frame our understanding of the entire mission around one B17 crew and its fears, failings and foibles. This framing device changes our perspective – and radically. Where Middlebrook adopts a perspective which documents the fates of all those caught up in the events of 17 August 1943, the director of *Memphis Belle* has arranged his narrative resources to ensure that our appreciation of this mission is framed according to the needs of the crew of *Memphis Belle*. And to be fair the director does this rather successfully. When I watch this film I admit that I find myself rooting for the crew. I feel this way, of course, because, like the occupants of the aircraft, I have been distanced from the fate of those who occupy the target below.

It has been suggested that what became *Memphis Belle* was devel- oped in response to an earlier pitch which sought funding to produce a film based upon Len Deighton's novel *Bomber*, which focused upon the Royal Air Force and its night-time campaign against Berlin. I think it is a great shame that no backer could be found for a film project based upon Deighton's text, for two reasons. First, *Bomber* was successfully developed as a radio play so I am confident that it would have trans- lated into a cinematic project. Second, and perhaps more importantly, *Bomber*, in both its book and play formats, is a profoundly anti-war text whereas *Memphis Belle*, despite the quality and intensity of its ariel combat sequences is framed rather differently. Thus *Memphis Belle*, when all is said and done, remains an heroic tale. It is, thanks to a framing device which focuses our attention upon a group of young American men, a celebration of death from above; a curious combination of the films *Summer Holiday* and *Spice World*.[1] It is, when all is said and done, a road-trip, a buddy movie; the story of an American boy-band and its European tour.

Focusing

The practices associated with the second F-factor, *focusing*, overlap to some degree with the account of *framing* outlined above, insofar as the development of a particular focal point necessarily limits the extent to which we may, for example, allow a frame that acknowledges the existence of other actors and/or other concerns. Thus it should be clear that (a) the decision to focus upon the activities of those within the B17 bomber named *Memphis Belle*, and (b) the dramatic arrangement of narrative resources which makes us inclined to root for these young men, tends to blind us to the fact that the success of this crew and, indeed, their continuing vitality, depends upon a rain of death and destruction. Recognising the overlap between our first two F-factors I will, if only for economy, consider Gabriel's third and fourth F-factors – *filtering* and *fading* – together.

Filtering and fading

Writing about his time spent in Marrakech, George Orwell (see Bott [1958] 1985) invites us to consider the manner in which we, often quite unwittingly, filter the world around us. Indeed in acknowledging the grinding poverty experienced by those then resident in this colony *and* in confronting the quiet but deep-seated racism that often excuses such conditions, Orwell demands that we recognise the ways in which our filtering practices can act to diminish the worlds and experiences of other humans; causing these poor individuals quite literally, as we shall see, to fade into the landscape:

> In northern Europe, when you see a labourer ploughing a field, you probably give him a second glance. In a hot country, anywhere south of Gibraltar or east of Suez, the chances are that you don't even see him. I have noticed this again and again. In a tropical landscape one's eyes take in everything except the human beings. It takes in the dried-up soil, the prickly pear, the palm trees and the distant mountain but it always misses the peasant hoeing at his patch ... For several weeks, always about the same time of day, [a]

file of old women had hobbled past the house with their firewood, and though they had registered themselves on my eyeballs I cannot truly say that I had seen them. Firewood was passing – that was how I saw it. It was only that one day I happened to be walking behind them, and the curious up-and-down motion of a load of wood drew my attention to the human being beneath it. Then for the first time I noticed the poor old earth-coloured bodies, bodies reduced to bones and leathery skin, bent double under the crushing weight. Yet I suppose I had not been five minutes on Moroccan soil before I noticed the overloading of the donkeys and was infuriated by it. There is no question that the donkeys are damnably treated. The Moroccan donkey is hardly bigger than a St. Bernard dog, it carries a load which in the British Army would be considered too much for a fifteen hands mule, and very often its pack saddle is not taken off its back for weeks together. But what is particularly pitiful is that it is the most willing creature on earth, it follows its master like a dog and does not need either bridle or halter. After a dozen years of devoted work it suddenly drops dead whereupon its master tips it into the ditch and the village dogs have torn its guts out before its cold.

This kind of thing makes one's blood boil, whereas – on the whole – the plight of the human being does not. I am not commenting, merely pointing to a fact. People with brown skins are next door to invisible. Anyone can be sorry for the donkey with its galled back but it is generally owing to some kind of accident if one even notices the old woman under her load of sticks.

(64–66)

In this passage Orwell seems to demand that we take some responsibility for the common practices of flitering and fading which allow us to feel the pain of donkeys and yet can scarcely acknowledge the presence of pitiful old women. Given this it is perhaps appropriate that I should take a few moments to reflect, personally, upon an episode which demonstrates only too well the manner in which I chose to filter the world around me and in so doing diminished the presence of others.

This recollected event includes two Scotsmen – myself and my brother's friend (whom we shall call Aird because that is his name and because my recollection will not in any way traduce his reputation); three young women and an overdue apology. As a preface to what will follow I would like to point out (a) that these events occurred almost 30 years ago, and (b) that – as the law courts have it – drink had been consumed. And with my plea of mitigation in place we can now turn to my recollection.

* * *

Some years ago I shared an apartment in Edinburgh with a few friends. I was enjoying pre-Christmas drinks with my flat-mates one mid-December evening when I bumped into my brother's friend, Aird. Following his graduation Aird had secured a management trainee position with the retailer Marks and Spencer and had, like me, retired to the pub to enjoy pre-Christmas drinks with his friends. Now at this stage of the tale my companions; my flat-mates, Rob, Anne and Kirsty will fade into the background and, to all intents and purposes, simply drop out of the narrative as we filter the events of the evening to allow me to focus upon those characters who are central to my tale.

I had been surprised to find Aird in this pub. Indeed I had been unaware of his presence in Edinburgh. I was, however, not at all surprised to learn that he had secured a position with Marks and Spencer since Aird enjoys the quiet self-confidence (and good looks) that graduate recruiters simply love.

After an initial exchange of (surprised) greetings, Aird introduced me to his three female companions and then departed for the bar to purchase another round of drinks. Left alone with three rather tall women, each of whom exhibited the characteristics preferred by graduate recruiters, I sought to engage in some small talk. I asked, knowing that Aird was now a trainee manager, if my absent friend was a 'good boss'.

In my defence I would add that I had based my inquiry upon empirical evidence: Marks and Spencer employs many women but its managerial ranks were then, at least, predominantly male. I would add, too, that Aird's companions responded courteously. Yet their reply soon made me wish that I might fade from the scene when it became apparent that I was, in fact, in the presence of Aird's bosses! If you recognise yourself in this tale more than 25 years on: I regret my assumptions. Indeed I am sorry still!

In an attempt to recover some social standing with you, the reader, I offer one more (vaguely) personal reflection on the practices of filtering and framing which will, I hope, demonstrate that maturity (and sobriety) have since improved the manner in which I construct and account for the world around me.

* * *

The discovery and development of penicillin as a medicine has had a transformative impact upon humanity. Few (young) people today fully recognise that prior to the discovery of penicillin, childbirth very often led to fatal complications. Indeed few people properly understand that in our pre-antibiotic world individuals would die of ailments and injuries that to our modern eye would appear trivial. Bryson (2014), for example, notes that the American tennis star Bill Tilden 'suffered an injury that should by any reckoning have ended his career' (133) in a pre-antibiotic world. Elaborating upon this point Bryson tells us:

> While playing in a tournament of absolutely no consequence in Bridgeton, New Jersey [Tilden] lunged for a ball and caught the middle finger of his racquet hand on the perimeter fence. The injury itself was trifling [but] two weeks later the top joint of the finger had to be amputated. Today the problem would be resolved with a course of antibiotics. In 1922 [Tilden] was lucky not to lose his arm, or even his life. (Calvin Coolidge's son would die from a similar infection the following year).
>
> (133)

As an Ayrshire man I take great pride in the fact that penicillin was discovered by Sir Alexander Fleming; a man who was born just a handful of miles from my own birthplace. Yet while most can volunteer the fact of penicillin's discovery, and while many might understand that this discovery was, in part, a product of Fleming's poor housekeeping. it would be wrong to cast Fleming as the lone genius who gifted penicillin to humankind. Thus while it is true that Fleming did indeed discover and did, first, document the antibiotic properties of the mould he had inadvertently cultured, it was in fact an Australian scientist, Howard Florey, and Ernest Chain, a refugee from Nazi Germany, who undertook the developmental work which allowed Fleming's penicillin to be manufactured as a medicine. The problem being, of course, that in so many renderings of this tale of 'discovery' the very significant contributions of Florey and Chain have been filtered in a manner which has caused these individuals to fade from public consciousness.

Fusing

Good storytellers understand those details that are central to their narratives. They also recognise those characters and events that are, consequently, marginal to the plot (my apologies Rob, Kirsty and Anne). In many cases the fusing processes which variously compress temporal differences or which act to remove characters from the stories rendered are fairly benign. Thus it is worth observing that when screenplays are developed from novels, events and characters are routinely cut to produce a cinematic experience that will not exhaust or otherwise try the patience of the audience. For example, the novel *Six Days of the Condor*, which was written by James Grady [1974] (2015) became *Three Days of the Condor* when it was released as a film starring Robert Redford in 1975.

Fitting

Memphis Belle works as a cinematic experience so long as we are inclined to accept that the crew of this B17 is engaged in a moral endeavour. To root for the crew, to hold on to the understanding that this is a group who deserve to fall in love, to get married and to grow old, we must be convinced that these young men are engaged in a precision attack against a legitimate military target. These requirements may go some way to explaining why – nationalist sentiments aside – US backers refused to fund a screenplay of *Bomber*. Thus we should acknowledge that the (imagined but not untypical RAF mission) which forms the centrepiece of *Bomber* was part of a broader 'area bombing' campaign designed to 'de-house' those involved in civilian forms of employment who were nonetheless deemed to be central to Germany's war efforts (see Harris [1947] 2005).

Storytellers who refuse to *fit* their work around the expectations of their audiences may find themselves treated roughly. In 1942 for example, John Steinbeck [1942] (1983) published a short novel set against the backdrop of Nazi Germany's invasion of Norway. Parini (1994) notes that an earlier draft of this manuscript which had imagined the occupation of a mid-sized American town by Nazi invaders was rejected by the commissioning agents (the Foreign Information Service or FIS) because it was thought that the text would spread feelings of 'defeatism'. Bruised by this experience, Parini tells us that Steinbeck reworked his text and in so doing chose to remove any obvious signifiers of place. Thus Parini notes that *The Moon is Down*, which was published soon after America entered the war in 1942, is set in an anonymous, European, coastal town which Steinbeck himself described as 'cold and stern like Norway, cunning and implacable like Denmark, reasonable like France. The names of the people I made as international as I could. I did not even call the Germans Germans, but simply invaders' (cited in Parini 1994: 316).

As he reworked the text of his novel Steinbeck worked hard to placate the sensibilities of his readers and, despite his own artistic instincts, altered his text to reflect the expectations of the broader public. But even these changes were not enough for everyone because while readers, it seems, would readily embrace the idea that good propaganda requires that we see something of ourselves in those who have been attacked, not all reviewers were inclined to indulge the idea that at least elements among the population of the invaders might also be 'polite', 'considerate and, at times, humane' (Parini 1994: 319).

Gabriel's '6F' factors usefully convey the manner in which poetic license is exercised and employed. Furthermore these F-factors suggest a clear distinction between stories and reportage which most casual observes would indulge. And yet further reflection suggests that much reporting actually builds and depends upon the resources more commonly associated with poetic tales.

Discussing inquiry reportage, Brown examines the official public inquiries which in Britain have been convened to investigate, respectively, an industrial accident (Brown 2000), a banking collapse (Brown 2005), harm to patients (Brown 2003) and ministerial misconduct (Brown and Jones 2000). He observes that as 'reports' these texts claim merely to chronicle events. Yet he argues that these documents patently, depend upon the artful arrangement of narratological resources as they attempt to develop satisfactory accounts of such events. In short Brown suggests that inquiry 'reports' are, at root, stories.

Building directly upon Brown's reflection, Collins et al. (2015) offer an account of the collapse of the Equitable Life, which considers the narrative resources available to those commissioned to conduct the inquiry into the failure of this mutual society. Observing that the official inquiry report on the Equitable affair depends upon the reader's acceptance that the chief executive of the Equitable Life was a Maxwellian[2] individual who knowingly and wilfully mismanaged the company for personal gain, Collins and his colleagues argue that this account of events remains unconvincing because it fails to marshal the narrative resources that will be required to construct a motive for the chief executive's supposedly Maxwellian conduct. Highlighting the extent to which the 'report' on the collapse of the Equitable Life depends upon those narrative resources more commonly associated with stories and storytelling, Collins et al. (2015) argue that the supposed 'Maxwellian' excesses of Equitable Life's chief executive are more usefully represented as a 'Micawberish' failure of capacity.[3] Offering a counterpoint to the story developed within the official inquiry report, therefore, Collins and his contemporaries note the attractions of the Maxwellian rendering of events (for example it makes the failure an individual pathology and in so doing safeguards the reputation of the industry and its regulators). Yet the authors argue that it makes more sense to suggest that the Equitable Life failed because its chief executive, like Wilkins Micawber, simply expected that Providence would intervene to reduce the widening gap between the society's assets and liabilities.

In the following section we will expand further upon the nature of that which is assumed to be merely reportage, as we consider the manner in which the events associated with Tianamen Square have been rendered and relayed to the general public. As we shall see, the reports which concern the events which unfolded in Tianamen Square in 1989 are peculiar because they transgress the normal conventions we associate with 'reporting'. Indeed, it is worth observing that reports of Tianamen Square have passed into history despite having no clear beginning, a disputed middle and an ending which fragments in its prematurity. Yet, I will attempt to demonstrate that these fragmenting reports can teach us much about the practice of storytelling. Furthermore, I will argue that our 're-view' of Tianamen offers key insights which should inform our attempts to put stories to work.

Reporting 'Tank Man'

Thanks to the reporting of the world's journalists most of us – at least those of us who do not reside in China – know of 'Tank Man' and Tianamen Square (Wright, 2000). As rendered by Western journalists, Tank Man's tale normally involves a young man, a main battle tank and a morally bankrupt regime. Yet this story has no clear beginning. It does have, however, what we might term 'a back-story' or broader context.

Reports of this incident typically begin with the observation that just after midday on the 5th of June 1989, a column of Norinco Type 69/59 main battle tanks was sighted on the Avenue of Eternal Peace in Beijing, China. In addition reports observe that this column was challenged by a young man who halted its progress. Yet to understand this incident we need to recognise the events which developed, more or less spontaneously, in early May.

During the month of May a group of students had staged a small demonstration in Tianamen Square, initially to demand an end to corruption. In a short time, however, this demonstration grew in both size and scope such that by the middle of the month Tianamen Square had been occupied by a large body of students, demanding dialogue with and democratic accountability from their leaders. During this period of occupation the students held debates and discussions. They constructed manifestoes, they carved a statue – the 'Goddess of

Democracy' – and to the surprise of many observers they enjoyed a limited dialogue with their leaders.

On the evening of the 4th of June, however, all this changed. The dialogue ceased abruptly and the Goddess of Democracy was smashed when the People's Liberation Army (PLA) entered Tiananmen Square in armoured personnel carriers. On that evening and during the night that followed many of the protestors were shot and killed as the PLA fired indiscriminately into the crowd.

On the following day a column of tanks was observed on the Avenue of Eternal Peace. As this column advanced one young man walked to the middle of the road and stopped in the path of the lead tank. This man had a bicycle with him and was carrying two small bags. The journalists who had been covering the demonstrations for some time were stunned by this man's actions. Trained in the mantra of journalism – *readers need to know who, what, when, where and why* – they speculated on the identity and occupation of this man. In the absence of more concrete information an identity was constructed. The man, it was agreed, was probably a student. His bags, it was suggested, contained books and perhaps a little something for lunch. A beginning to the story suggested itself: This man, whom some have called 'Tank Man' (Wright, 2000) had been in the square on the 4th of June when the government's soldiers began to shoot at the demonstrators and now, on his way home from the library, he had been shocked to see the tanks. Quite why someone who had seen his friends killed only the night before would have gone quietly to the library with a packed lunch in his hand remains unclear. But this beginning, for the moment, is good enough, given that the middle parts of our tale are also open to dispute.

So now we have a beginning: Tank Man is a mild-mannered student, an ordinary man studying for a degree, who finds himself in the middle of the road facing down a column of battle tanks because he can no longer tolerate the violence and corruption of his rulers. Transformed from a man of letters into a man of action, Tank Man confronts the tank column.

As the tanks approached the world's media looked on. Tank Man did not move. Perhaps he held his breath. Perhaps he closed his eyes and prepared to face death. What would you do?

If you plan to tell this story yourself you may wish to invite your audience to consider this question. Indeed, if you yourself hope to use this story to inform and to entertain you may wish to act upon this opportunity for embellishment. So I ask again: What would you do?

As the vehicle bore down on Tank Man it faltered and then stopped. The tracked vehicle then began to turn to its right, but Tank Man altered his position to block its progress. It then veered to the left, but

Tank Man again turned to obstruct it, all the time shouting and gesturing to the occupants. When the tank stopped again, the lone protestor climbed on to the body of the vehicle and continued to harangue the occupants. Eventually a man (assumed to be the tank's commander) emerged from the turret and a short exchange took place. Minutes later, Tank Man departed the scene and the tanks continued their menacing procession for a further 120 yards or so, until they were confronted once more by their tormentor. After another few minutes others (assumed to be fellow students and protestors) intervened and, after some persuasion, Tank Man was led away, leaving the tanks free to proceed.

Wright (2000) notes that photographs and video clips of this 'mechanical ballet' were soon beamed to a worldwide audience. The journalists who provided the text of this encounter were struck by Tank Man's bravery and by his willingness to take a stand, alone. Yet none of those who reported the events have any clue about what passed between Tank Man and the tank's commander. The reporters (nearly) present at this scene, we should note, witnessed the events from balconies far away and through long lenses. Despite this separation, however, the world's journalists chose to celebrate Tank Man as a hero and encouraged their viewers and listeners to do the same.

And who could blame the press for coming to this conclusion? In the face of a violent and authoritarian regime Tank Man had had the courage to confront a 40-ton weapon of war. Using force of will and strength of character he had stopped a tank column. Tank Man, it was agreed, was an inspiration to us all.

Yet, as we noted, the middle of our tale is disputed. Indeed, Deng Xiaoping suggested that the tale of Tank Man has been distorted by Western propaganda. In an attempt to unsettle such propaganda, Chairman Deng's rendering of this tale introduces a larger cast of characters. Deng's story re-casts Tank Man as 'a scoundrel' bringing disorder to China and introduces a new hero to the cast-list. For Deng the true heroes of this encounter are the People's Liberation Army (PLA), for he reasons that Tank Man could not have stopped the tanks. The PLA, he argues, could easily have continued down the eight-lane highway which is the Avenue of Eternal Peace, but they exercised restraint in the face of this scoundrel's protests.

Given the activities of the 4th of June it is difficult to view the PLA as heroes. Indeed it is difficult to suppress a sardonic grin when confronted with the medal that was struck to recognise the soldiers', *ahem*, heroism. Yet, Deng's attempt to spin this encounter is instructive nonetheless. In challenging the Western media's depiction of Tank

Man, Deng introduces a wider cast of characters and concerns, which begin to fragment and disrupt what has been up to this point a rather stable and familiar story. Quite paradoxically, in fact, Deng's attempt to bolster an authoritarian regime invites us to make space for alternative and more local renderings of the Tank Man tale, because it encourages us to consider the actions of a small number of young men within the lead tank who have hitherto been ignored by the tellers of Tank Man's tale(s).

In a story where so little can be known with certainty, one thing is clear. History records that the tank stopped. But who stopped the tank? Journalists struck by the drama of the moment and by the poetics of their trade have suggested that Tank Man stopped the column. Yet this is not quite true. While Tank Man clearly obstructed the path of the vehicles, he did not stop them. Within the lead tank someone must have taken a decision not to proceed. Acknowledging the bravery of Tank Man, Wright (2000) nonetheless wonders if it might be wise to 'write-in' parts for the tank crew implicated in our drama. Indeed, Wright suggests that the tank's commander may well be the real hero of the tale because he ordered the tank driver to stop.

So how does the tale end? Having fabricated a beginning and been offered a choice of 'middles' and casts you are, for the time being, at liberty to select your own hero and your own ending!

Perhaps you are comfortable with the tale preferred by Western journalism. Perhaps you will side with Deng. Perhaps your 'ending' will follow Tank Man as a hero. Perhaps you will follow him as a scoundrel. Perhaps you will focus on the tank's commander. But whatever route you choose, one thing is surely clear: The reports of Tank Man and his interactions with a column of tanks on the Avenue of Eternal Peace make sense only if we are prepared to indulge the '6Fs' of storytelling which we tend to assume are denied those whom we entrust to bring us the news. Thus it should be clear that the familiar account of the events of 5 June 1989 holds together only if we are willing to accept that, despite being perched on balconies high above the Avenue of Eternal Peace, the journalists reporting these events were close enough to the actors and the interactions that took place between those involved that they could simply chronicle what transpired.

When discussing the events of 5 June 1989 with students and corporate executives, I often explore the limits of this chronicle by mischievously suggesting that what has gone down in history as a political act on a par with, say, Rosa Park's public refusal to give up her seat or the quieter refusal of Richard and Mildred Loving to abandon their marriage (see the *Economist*, 15 May 2008), might actually have been a romantic affair. Thus I often suggest that we have intruded on a private moment involving a tank commander, a student and a young woman, not present at the scene, who is nonetheless the subject of their joint affections. This narrative has, I think, certain merits. By casting Tank Man as a romantically thwarted, but apolitical student, for example, we can enact a world wherein our scholar might well have packed his lunch and visited the library on the morning of 5 June. Indeed, to add texture and colour to this narrative (a theme to which we will later return) I sometimes suggest that the ardour of the young men in the tale is made altogether more intense because they have fallen for a woman who is tall, beautiful, clever, funny ... and local to Beijing. Thus I suggest that this romantic tryst has a special significance because future marriage will convey residential privileges to whichever of these country boys is able to convince the woman to accept their declarations of undying love.

Deep down of course I am more inclined to accept a politicised version rather than the romantic rendering of 'Tianamen' proffered above. And while I have no wish, either, to deny or to trivialise the murderous events of 4 June 1989, it is nevertheless pertinent to suggest that we do not actually know what passed between those who participated in this otherwise very public drama and we will, I suspect, never truly 'know'. Furthermore, we would do well to remember that it is in these spaces that the wonder, the beauty and the power of storytelling are truly revealed.

And with this thought in mind we will now examine a debate as to the essential characteristics of poetic tales. Having navigated a passage through this debate we will conclude this chapter by considering the manner in which narrative resources might be constituted and arranged to produce different story-forms.

The essence of stories

A number of authors have attempted to codify the essence of stories (see Czarniawska 1997; Søderberg 2003). Gabriel (2000; 2004) offers perhaps the most comprehensive of these codifications (see Collins 2007). Drawing upon Aristotle's (1965) classical formulation Gabriel argues that stories – properly so-called – exhibit a number of key characteristics. Stories, he tells us:

- involve characters in a predicament
- unfold according to a chain of events that, in turn, reflects the structure of the plot and the essential traits of the characters involved

- call upon symbolism/symbolic factors
- indulge poetic embellishment and narrative embroidery
- have a beginning, middle and end
- seek to convey not simple facts but more general and enduring truths.

Teasing out the significance of this final, discriminating factor, Gabriel tells us that:

> stories purport to relate to facts that happened, but also discover in these facts a plot or meaning, by claiming that facts do not merely happen but that they happen in accordance with the requirements of a plot. In short, stories are not 'just fictions' (although they may be fictions), nor are they mere chronologies of events as they happened. Instead, they represent poetic elaborations of narrative material, aiming to communicate *facts as experience,* not facts as information.
>
> (Gabriel 2004: 64, original emphasis)

Greatbatch and Clark (2005), however, take issue with the 'classical' account of storytelling (see Aristotle 1965) preferred by Gabriel. It is worth taking just a few moments to explore this challenge. Yet as we commence our critical reflections on the 'inductive' account of storytelling (Collins 2012a; 2013) developed by these authors we should concede that this analysis is embedded within an account of management's gurus which is actually rather insightful. Thus Greatbatch and Clark suggest that academic and journalistic commentaries on management's gurus focus, narrowly, upon what gurus *write* but in so doing neglect to consider what these gurus *say* and *do* in their public seminars.

Reflecting upon the stories that gurus (see Huczynski 1993) render in their seminars, Greatbatch and Clark usefully highlight:

a   the role which non-verbal communication plays in the performance work undertaken by management's gurus
b   the interactive quality of the seminars offered by the gurus
c   the manner in which humour – and its response: laughter – is employed to manage audience affiliation.

In addition Greatbatch and Clark remind us of:

a   the vulnerability of the performer, and
b   the precarious nature of his/her performance.

These are important insights which we will return to as we attempt to realise the power of talk in organizations. Yet while noting the manner in which the broader insights of Greatbatch and Clark might be used to guide our storytelling endeavours, we must nonetheless acknowledge the perverse manner in which the authors attempt to define poetic tales.

Greatbatch and Clark (2005), like Gabriel (2000), observe an increase in the number of academic studies concerned with the nature and function of organizational stories, yet they choose to mount a challenge to what they see as the emerging orthodoxy on storytelling. Thus Greatbatch and Clark protest that the literature on organizational storytelling is flawed insofar as it privileges the researcher's viewpoint. Indeed, they complain that academic accounts of organizational storytelling proceed from an understanding that is predicated upon 'a priori formal definitions' (110) of narrative form.

In an attempt to undermine what the authors clearly regard as a deterministic approach to storytelling, Greatbatch and Clark suggest that stories should be defined from the perspective of the listener.[4] Challenging the logic that underpins the storytelling approaches of commentators such as Aristotle (1965), Martin et al. (1983), Boje (1991), Gabriel (2000) and Søderberg (2003), therefore, Greatbatch and Clark (2005) suggest that stories are defined not by form but by proclamation.

Stressing the importance of this bugle call, Greatbatch and Clark (2005) tell us that from their perspective as researchers, 'a segment of talk that is classifiable as a "story" is projected as a story by the teller so that it comes off as a story for the hearer' (110). And they add:

> The gurus have to indicate that they are about to tell a story so that the members of the audience hear what is being presented as a story.
> (110)

There is, however, a basic tension in this attempt to reconfigure the academic analysis of storytelling. Recognising the extent to which the performing storyteller is dependent upon and therefore vulnerable in the face of her audience, Greatbatch and Clark (2005) are obliged to qualify their initial statement on the nature of storytelling. Thus they argue that any segment of talk which is announced as a tale must also be 'recognizable and hearable as a story' (110).

But how can the authors know that what has been announced as a story has, in fact, been recognised and heard in these terms? It may be helpful to consider the materials surveyed by Greatbatch and Clark as we respond to this question.

Storytelling in guru seminars

The accounts of guru performance developed by Greatbatch and Clark (2005) draw upon commercially available recordings. These video materials, we should note, have been produced with a specific purpose in mind: They are designed (ostensibly) as aids to staff training and development. Consequently the camera tends to focus its attention upon the guru and the stage that s/he occupies. The audience, therefore, appears on screen irregularly and only fleetingly. Indeed for the most part the audience in these recordings exists offstage in a darkened auditorium and reminds us of its presence only periodically through the sound of its laughter and, less frequently, the noise of its applause. Greatbatch and Clark acknowledge this limitation. They cannot, they tell us, account for speaker–audience interactions on a moment-by-moment basis because the audience and the stage seldom appear on screen together. Yet despite this the authors continue to assume that they know (a) what the audience can hear, (b) what it can recognise, and (c) what it will choose to hear as a story. Thus Greatbatch and Clark (2005) inform us that 'Peters told 12 stories' (112) in the seminar extracts they analysed. However their own account of storytelling makes it plain that Peters' willingness to announce a story is a necessary but not sufficient condition for this form of exchange. So how can the authors be assured that what Peters projects as a story constitutes a segment of talk that is, from the perspective of the audience, 'recognizable and hearable' in these terms?

In reply Greatbatch and Clark may choose to argue that the response of the audience will signal that a segment of talk has, in fact, been heard as a story. This method, I concede, may work for some stories. For example audience laughter in response to a segment of talk projected as a humorous tale could, reasonably, be taken as a signal that the audience has *recognised and heard* a funny story. But what should we make of silence? Not all stories are funny. Some are designed to move us in different ways. Indeed some stories are designed to precipitate a sudden interest in the floor beneath us! So what should we make of those segments of talk that are projected as stories yet fail to precipitate a vocal response from the audience? Do these projections remain stories or do they have to be classified in other terms?

Greatbatch and Clark provide no response to these questions. And their failure to address these issues demonstrates that their preferred approach simply cannot provide an adequate means of framing story-telling. Thus the bald assertion that 'Peters told 12 stories' (Greatbatch and Clark 2005: 112) makes sense, only, if we accept that the authors can know in advance what an audience might find 'hearable' as a story.

Yet Greatbatch and Clark rule out this presumption. Indeed, they insist that this approach to organizational storytelling would be high-handed and deterministic!

So what does the 'inductive' approach to storytelling preferred by Greatbatch and Clark actually reveal about the power of talk in organizations? Not very much I fear: Greatbatch and Clark place storytelling at the heart of their analysis of performance. This is perfectly sensible. They assert furthermore that stories are the very fulcrum upon which audiences are moved. This, too, is perfectly sensible and resonates with the central theme of this text. Yet the approach adopted by the authors all but prevents the sensible analysis of storytelling, insofar as it rejects and yet seems to require a classical definition of the poetic tale. Little wonder, then, that in recent forays into the world of guru performance Clark (Clark et al. 2012; Groβ et al. 2015) chooses, *quietly*, to drop his inductive account of storytelling and – without further elaboration or explanation – simply reverts to the classical or deductive approach that he had previously defamed (see Collins 2012a; 2013). Later we will suggest that successful storytellers establish narratives that are, both, plausible and consistent. For the moment, however, we will linger to consider the poetic tropes.

The poetic tropes

Just a few moments' reflection should reveal that not all stories are alike. As we noted above, some stories make us laugh. Some make us cry. Others make us angry. Some may render us dumbfounded. How do storytellers and, more importantly, how might you manufacture these outcomes within organized settings?

Gabriel (2000; see also Tietze et al. 2003) argues that storytellers call upon 'poetic tropes' or generic attributions as they attempt to make events meaningful. Outlining these poetic tropes, Gabriel suggests that poetic tropes are the attributes which breathe life into stories, and so give them the capacity to communicate experience. Poetic or proper stories, therefore, tend to attribute:

1   motive – which, for example, defines events to be accidental or incidental;
2   causal connections – which outline the cause and effects of actions;
3   responsibility – where blame and credit are allocated to actors and actions;
4   unity – such that a group comes to be defined as such;
5   fixed qualities – such that heroes are heroic and villains, villainous;

6   emotion – to describe the emotional characteristics of actions;
7   agency – whereby volition is variously raised or diminished;

And finally, Gabriel draws our attention to:

8   providential significance – which is especially important in certain tales, for example where higher forms of being – gods, angels, super-heroes or wizards – intervene to restore justice and order.

Gabriel observes that authors may structure the poetic tropes to produce a number of different 'poetic modes', designed variously to inculcate pride in, or to bring laughter forth from, the enraptured listener. Documenting the main poetic modes, Gabriel suggests that a tale may be (a) comic, (b) tragic, (c) epic, or (d) romantic, depending upon the construction and organization of characters and events. It is important to note, however, that Gabriel's terminology departs somewhat from the traditional labels used to define storytelling tropes. Thus in the analysis of Shakespearean works, for example, 'comic' tales are those that conclude with an upturn in the hero's fortunes whereas 'tragic' tales conclude with a down-turn in our hero's prospects. In contrast, Gabriel's 'comic' tales are humorous in outcome and intent. Thus for Gabriel comic tales precipitate laughter whereas 'tragic' tales are said to generate sadness. 'Epic' tales, in contrast, typically concern the lives and endeavours of remarkable figures. Consequently these stories tend to have simple and rather linear plot-lines. Indeed, epic tales generally devote little time to the intricacies and complexities of character development. Instead these stories focus upon action, movement, achievement and closure as they encourage us to admire the accomplishments of the special individual who has been placed at the very centre of the drama (Collins and Rainwater 2005).

Before we attempt to unleash the power of that special form of 'talk' that is organizational storytelling it will be useful to consider in more detail the characteristics of the epic, comic romantic and tragic forms as these are now commonly constituted, so that we might then consider the arrangement of narrative resources required in order to conjure and to sustain these narrative forms.

The arrangement of narrative resources

In an attempt to develop a more concrete understanding of narrative form *and* an appreciation of the arrangement of narrative resources which is required in order to create and sustain the epic, the comic, the romantic and the tragic form, we will now consider four films. Two of these films are very well known; one is perhaps less familiar, and another (the romantic) is a stereotyped and a more-or-less imagined projection of my own particular preferences and prejudices. These brief reflections, however, will provide useful, practical guidance on the arrangement of narrative resources that you might utilise to refine your own storytelling practices.

To illustrate the epic form I have chosen the film *Star Wars*. This film is so familiar that I do not feel the need to recount its plot. Moreover I do not intend to engage in a discussion of whether Episode IV is superior to Episode I (although it almost certainly is). Nor will I entertain invitations to discuss whether Jar Jar Binks blights the franchise (although he certainly does). Instead I will consider the narrative resources that shape and define this epic tale.

Building upon a pro forma suggested by Gabriel (2000) and later applied by Collins and Rainwater (2005), the film *Star Wars* may be considered to be an epic tale which involves:

A protagonist	Luke Skywalker
A rescue object	The Republic
Assistants	Han Solo, Princess Leia, Chewie and Obi Wan among others

In a noble quest that is built around:

A predicament	How to defeat the evil empire and in so doing restore democracy and self-determination to any number of conquered worlds.

To advance and sustain this tale we need to embrace some model of constitutional democracy; how else can we juxtapose democracy and royalty? In addition we need to focus the attention of the audience upon:

Agency	The rebels, despite the obvious risks and despite the odds, refuse to accept their continuing subjugation. In short they rebel.
Motive	This epic tale has a romantic sub-plot of course but at root the key motivation of Luke and his assistants is to defeat the evil that is the empire, and so, restore democracy and self-determination.
Credit	Primarily credit flows to Luke because (spoiler alert!) he uses 'the force' to destroy the 'Death Star'.
Fixed qualities	Our heroes are brave and despite the odd hiccup and argument they are, when all is said and done, loyal and steadfast.

The successful arrangement of these resources leads to a dramatic conclusion which produces key emotions, namely pride and admiration, both for Luke and for our better selves. Although, and without wishing to detract from what is a rather wonderful film, I have always wondered about the values of a society which would decorate Luke, Chewie and Han for their bravery and yet ignore the contribution of their obviously sentient robot helpers!

To illustrate the comic form, I have chosen the film *Shallow Hal*. I have chosen this film because it is well known and because it has Anthony Robbins[5] (a self-help guru of quite extraordinary proportions) in a cameo role.

In *Shallow Hal* Jack Black plays the eponymous hero. Due to what the lawyers for Tiger Woods would term 'an adverse reaction to prescription medicine', Hal forms a stunted appreciation of the opposite sex which is notable for its objectification. Consequently Hal's romantic relationships are shallow, dysfunctional and short-lived.

At root *Shallow Hal* is a physical comedy which arranges scenes and events to mock Hal and his shallow objectification of women. It is worth noting, however, that when Hal is released from this overly-sexualised trap the tables are turned and we are invited to share in the film's mockery of society's preference for (shallow) beauty above the deeper qualities that flow from character and kindness.

Shallow Hal is, I think, pretty funny. But it is worth reminding ourselves that it secures its comedic effect because of the manner in which it arranges its narrative resources. Thus it casts:

A foolish protagonist	Shallow Hal, who, it is worth observing, is also the plot's rescue object.
Assistants	Hal's friends who variously enable and less often challenge his objectification of women. In addition, Anthony Robbins appears in a cameo role and uses *mystical* powers to unleash Hal's as-yet-untapped ability to see the deeper beauty in the women around him.

In a tale of comic misadventure which visits misfortune, indignity and ultimately the capacity for change upon Hal as it deals with:

A predicament	Hal is blocked; his preferences and predilections allow him to choose wisely and without prejudice when it comes to male friends Yet he is unable to secure romantic fulfilment with those women whom he finds physically attractive.

To reveal this problem and to secure Hal's redemption within a comedic frame, the film needs to shape our appreciation of Hal's character and predicament in terms of:

Agency	Robbins frees our hero but Hal soon reveals himself to be a worthy rescue object because he demonstrates that he is, in fact, capable of deep and lasting change.
Motive	Hal wants to be happily in love.
Credit	Robbins enables Hal's initial development but most of the credit, it becomes clear, belongs to Hal.
Fixed qualities	Hal is initially vain and distracted but his same-sex relationship choices allow us to see that he is, at root, a good person albeit one who has, in the words of the poet Philip Larkin, been 'fucked up' by his parents.

The successful management of these resources produces a pleasing, funny narrative, albeit one which does tend to indulge a number of rather conventional 'fat jokes' while ostensibly challenging notions of objectification.

The third film I have chosen to discuss does not exist in a concrete and specific sense but it does, I suggest, exist at a more general level albeit as a stereotyped product of my prejudiced imagination. This 'film', which I will call *Sad Bob Finds a Bride*, has similarities with the core plot and key concerns of *Shallow Hal*. Yet where *Shallow Hal* is comedic, *Sad Bob Finds a Bride* is a romantic melodrama which involves:

A protagonist	A beautiful woman.
A rescue object	'Sad Bob', who is strong, silent and distant. The reasons for this distant silence are pretty much interchangeable and include, amongst other things, being jilted at the altar; being betrayed by a friend; the death of his spouse, either suddenly and violently, or after a long illness during which Bob acted as both nurse and lover. For this 'film' you may take your pick. So for present purposes let's agree that Bob is sad because his wife died after a long illness but that he now needs to move on with the help of the beautiful women listed above … because his wife (whom he loved truly) would not have wanted him to mourn for evermore.

To allow this outline plot to develop and to proceed to a satisfactory conclusion, the audience for my imagined movie will need to indulge the artful arrangement of key narrative resources:

Agency	Bob must demonstrate that he is able to overcome the predispositions which make him quiet, distant, aloof and immune to the romantic overtures that would, if only he could loosen up, redeem him.
Motive	The beautiful woman hatches a plan to redeem Bob from his self-imposed romantic exile.
Credit	Thanks to 'the beautiful woman' and Bob's friends, we are able to celebrate the development of a newly happy and romantically fulfilled Bob.
Fixed qualities	We have known all along that Bob is decent and kind; he loved and nursed his wife and has many functioning platonic friendships. As the movie concludes, therefore, Bob is once again in a position where he can be open to the romantic love that will complete and fulfil him.

The successful arrangement of these resources produces, if not an Oscar winner then a perfectly agreeable romantic narrative; a soppy feeling and – for men – protestations that they have 'just got something in my eye'.

The final form I have chosen to discuss is the tragic form. Where the comic form is designed to precipitate laughter, and where the epic form is arranged to solicit pride and admiration, the tragic form is designed to generate feelings of sorrow and/or indignation. The film I have chosen to illustrate the tragic narrative form is *Inside Job*, a documentary which examines the financial crash of 2008. This film claims to produce a broadly factual chronicle of the events of autumn 2008 and does so pretty effectively. But its status as a documentary does not mean that it is somehow freed from a requirement to secure the artful arrangement of narrative resources. Indeed, we could argue that the film achieves its intended effect – to make us angry and indignant – precisely because it develops, arranges and deploys an array of narrative resources that by now should be pretty familiar. Thus *Inside Job* is a tragedy which involves:

A protagonist	One or a number of hard-working families whose dreams and aspirations are threatened.
A villainous presence	Wall Street and the greedy 'fat cats' who have destroyed the banking system, and consequently the very foundations of the economy.

In a tragic tale which deals with:

A predicament	How to keep home and family together in a context that is both literally and metaphorically bankrupt.

To develop our appreciation of this predicament and our indignation, the film employs:

Agency	The architects and custodians of the global financial system have managed its processes and outcomes in a manner that is now shown to be reckless and selfish.
Motive	Those ordinary folk who have purchased homes, pensions and financial services, more generally, need to find some means of surviving the acts of the agents noted above.
Credit	In truth no one apart from the film-makers comes out of this well, although some are painted more sympathetically than others. Thus 'the bankers' are portrayed as venal and the regulators, it is suggested, plainly lack competence. Meanwhile those who purchased financial services are presented as a bit naïve and as being rather easily sold.
Fixed qualities	The ordinary workers and their families are noble – if naïve. The bankers are greedy and the regulators and politicians who were charged with oversight are and will remain feckless.

The successful arrangement of these resources produces a narrative that provokes feelings of sadness and indignation among the intended audience.

You should now have a more developed appreciation of the ways in which narrative resources may be arranged to produce useful and meaningful outcomes. As you prepare to craft and share stories within your workplace you may find it useful to use some version of this pro forma to ensure that your storytelling (a) remains plausible, (b) remains consistent, and (c) promotes the forms of thought and action that you would prefer.

In an attempt to enable your use of this pro forma and in so doing facilitate your pursuit of useful narrative outcomes, our next chapter offers six sets of questions. These questions, as we shall see, have been designed to refine your storytelling practices, because whether or not you care to concede it, shaping the thoughts and actions of those around you is a rather testing endeavour.

Notes

1 *Summer Holiday* is a film starring the ever-young British pop star Cliff Richard. The film imagines a European holiday undertaken by a group of British teenagers (when such travel was still unusual) aboard an iconic

London double-decker bus. *Spiceworld* is a pop mockumentary (a pale reflection of *Spinal Tap*) which follows the Spice Girls on tour.

2 Robert Maxwell was a British MP, publisher and newspaper owner whose name has become synonymous with corporate criminality.

3 Wilkins Micawber is a character created by Charles Dickens. Micawber understands and proclaims the importance of fiscal self-discipline but is, tragically, unable to live up to his own maxim.

4 This is, of course, a very powerful assertion. In their *Dictionary of Sociology*, Abercrombie et al. (1994) note that determinism is 'usually a term of abuse in sociology' (113).

5 Amongst other trials and challenges designed to improve the confidence and capabilities of his students, Robbins has his followers engage in a fire-walking trial. This is presented as a 'mind over matter' challenge. However even a rudimentary understanding of the concept of 'specific heat capacity' demonstrates that 'fire-walking' is in fact a rather trivial, low-risk, undertaking. As the father of two children I will become convinced when Robbins can allow me to walk unscathed across Lego bricks.

5 Putting stories to work

So far we have established that organizational storytelling is usefully understood as a response to the political problems and emotional complexities associated with shaping and directing the efforts of others. In addition we have considered the ways in which managers have been encouraged to regard stories as tools that can be used to secure control over the processes which shape thought and action at work. Examining sensemaking and sensegiving processes, we have reflected upon the different ways in which such accounts (a) conceptualise the essence of social organization, (b) construct stories, and (c) project the capacity of storytelling at work. In addition we have considered the manner in which poetic tropes may be arranged to produce different forms and effects. And at this point critical academic commentary tends to tail off. But I am not quite ready to shamble back to the common room.[1] Indeed I believe that without causing too much violence to the ethos of 'critical scholarship' (see Parker and Thomas 2011; Butler and Spoelstra 2012) it should be possible to say something useful, something productive, about the practices and processes associated with telling tales at work. To this end I offer six headline questions or, perhaps more accurately, six sections of talk designed to encourage further reflection and action on organizational storytelling.

1 What do I want to achieve?

If we accept that the special form of talk known as storytelling has a capacity to shape thought and action within organized settings, then it seems sensible to suggest that in your attempts to control and co-ordinate the efforts of others you should take steps to ensure that the stories you produce actually promote the mode of thought and the forms of conduct that you believe to be necessary. Of course, those who endorse a sensemaking account of storytelling generally insist that stories are more complex and more fragile than most managers allow. None-theless, it seems clear that if you choose to tell a story which fails to communicate your core intentions you will license interactions and forms of conduct that may be contrary to your aims. Putting this more succinctly: If you want to improve 'quality' in your workplace do make sure that your storytelling repertoire does not focus narrowly upon 'quantity'!

So as you announce a story, as you invite those around you to sus-pend the normal rules of conversational exchange, you may wish to pause for a moment so that you might first ask yourself:

> Does my story reliably communicate the patterns of thought and action that I would like my friends, colleagues, stakeholders and/or co-workers to adopt?

2 Given my intended audience, are my stories actually plausible?

Stories are, as we have established, 'world building' endeavours (Latour 1987; Weick 1995). Or more plainly: In an organizational context stories are attempts to construct and to legitimate particular ways of thinking, feeling and acting. Stories, in short, have the potential to cause and allow change.

Yet any change that you might seek to foster in future will build from what *is* now. So even as you attempt to reorientate your collea-gues, your employees and/or your customers through storytelling, you must remain sensitive to the immanent quality of social organization. Furthermore you must remain sensitive to the dilemmas and tensions that structure daily life, because it is these elements of our organized existence that will surely structure organizational storytelling (from the bottom up).

Martin and her colleagues (Martin et al. 1983) capture this rather well. They observe that most organizations claim to be unique in cul-tural terms. Additionally they observe that when organizational mem-bers are asked to account for these assertions of uniqueness they tend to warrant their claims through storytelling. Yet when these stories are compared across different organizations they are found to be remark-ably similar. Reflecting upon these storytelling practices, Martin et al. (1983) suggest that seven key story-types tend to feature across a diverse range of organizations. Accounting for this finding, the authors suggest that these tales are constructed, and through repeated telling, are maintained within organizations because they reflect the persistent anxieties that are associated with the experience of working. Thus

Martin et al. suggest that, otherwise, diverse organizations possess similar storyworlds because employees experience common anxieties in the face of power structures designed, variously, to control their interactions and to discipline their conduct.

In my own research (Collins 2013) I have examined Tom Peters' storytelling in the light of the analysis developed by Martin et al. (1983). I suggest that there are clear differences between the story-worlds constructed by Peters and those documented by Martin and her colleagues. Tom Peters' storyworld, for example, seeks to narrate the organization from the 'top down' whereas Martin and her colleagues have explored the construction of social organization from the 'bottom up'. Furthermore my research suggests that there is often a rupture between storytelling practices employed at the top of the organization and the stories that circulate towards the bottom of the organization. Indeed, I argue that Peters' storyworld lacks plausibility because it completely ignores a persistent and, increasingly, common anxiety in relation to *insecurity*.

So before you tell your colleagues, your employees, your suppliers, or even your customers a tale, first ask yourself:

Is my story plausible?

Do the stories I tell reflect or acknowledge the persistent anxi-eties associated with working? Do my stories, for example, take account of the specific stressors that my demands for service, for commitment and for professionalism, more generally, place upon employees and/or colleagues?

Or, more simply, do my stories appreciate the problems and processes of work as these are experienced towards the bottom of the pyramid?

3 Are my storytelling practices unwittingly exclusionary?

My research on storytelling practices (Collins and Rainwater 2005; Collins 2007; 2008) suggests that epic tales of organizational endeavour tend dominate the publications that are aimed at practising managers. Greatbatch and Clark (2005), of course, suggest that in their seminar performances, gurus tend to lean more heavily on comic narratives. Nonetheless, it remains true that journals such as the *Harvard Business Review* and *Sloan Management Review*, which in effect set the tone of managerial discourse, trade exclusively in a form of organizational storytelling which details and demands a commitment to the organi-zation that is single-minded and unwavering. The problem being, of course, that the lives of employees are more complex and rather more fractured than this narrative formation generally allows. As I draft this manuscript on a chilly but bright February afternoon, for example, I do so with one eye on the clock. My wife is at work but like many female employees she works during 'term time' to ensure that she is available to look after our children when they are released from school for the vacation periods. Yet since my wife is at work and will today remain at her desk long after the school day finishes, I must endure the school run. So any minute now I will need, temporarily, to abandon my writing. Few organizational tales, however, countenance the school run, or, indeed, acknowledge the existence of dependants or even children in the wider society.

I explored the (unacknowledged) context of working – somewhat less biographically – in a paper which examined the presence and position of women in the organizational storyworld of a leading guru (see Collins 2012a). My research suggests that managerial storytelling insofar as it depends upon 'epic' story-forms is exclusionary because such tales project the need for a form of organizational commitment which asserts that core elements of the workforce – women, parents, carers, etc. – are not and cannot hope to be full organizational members.

So before you next tell a story that you hope will reorient and reanimate others, think for a moment about the stories that you have recently crafted and employed. Think also of the character of those tales that you tend to repeat. How many of these tales, for example, acknowledge the presence of women in the workplace? And how many acknowledge the broader context (of work, family and home) that shapes the contribution of women, carers and parents at work?

If your stories do not at least index these issues and concerns you have a problem; a problem I suggest that can only be addressed by developing a new storyworld.

4 Do I actually live up to the practical or behavioural exemplars that feature in my stories?

Some years ago when I was a young and very junior member of the academic community I gratefully accepted a post at the University of Essex. Soon after I took up my employment the director of research at that time (who shall remain nameless) invited me to meet him in his office in order to discuss my research. I was aware that this was – as *Mafiosi* phrase it – 'an offer that I could not refuse', and so, I was careful to prepare an engaging narrative around my research that might proclaim my awesomeness (I did warn you that I was a lot younger at the time!).

Yet I need not have bothered. You see, despite the fact that the meeting had been scheduled to discuss *my* research, I spoke no more than two words during the whole encounter. *And it lasted fully 45 minutes.* I was, however, treated to an extended review of my research director's career, which demonstrated to his satisfaction at least that it was he who was awesome!

Before too long this research director was succeeded by another professorial colleague. To my great relief this individual did not invite me to attend a meeting to discuss my research. Instead he paid me a compliment insofar as he asked me to comment upon a paper concerned with 'narrative' that he had been trying to develop. But I don't want to linger on this story. I have a better tale to tell!

My new research director had, at that time, a mature Ph.D. student. This student placed considerable demands upon my colleague's time, and since he guarded this jealously, she was deemed to be problematic.

The student in question, it seems, had recently taken to turning up at my colleague's office for impromptu and largely unproductive meetings. To forestall this unwelcome initiative my research director had developed an expedient and, initially, productive response: Whenever he heard this student approaching he would hide under his desk. On entering the office the troublesome student would find it unoccupied, would shrug her shoulders, and promptly depart the scene. Or I should say that this is the situation that prevailed until one fateful day when, instead of shrugging and departing she decided to have a seat to await the return of her noble mentor. On that humid midsummer afternoon, my senior colleague was obliged to crouch silently beneath his desk for around 35 minutes until his troublesome student returned to her familiar pattern of behaviour and departed.

These stories about the vanities and failings of my erstwhile research directors still make me smile. But I have a serious point to make: While you are busy crafting tales of (your) epic endeavours, what stories are your colleagues and co-workers telling of you? Are you a hero or a zero? I guess that you are, like me, somewhere in-between. Given this, I suggest that you may wish to think more carefully about how you cast your tales in future.

John Steinbeck captures this rather well and, once more, offers useful guidance to the managerial storyteller. During World War II Steinbeck worked as a war correspondent in the European theatre of operations (and in later life performed a similar function in Vietnam – see Barden 2012).

Steinbeck was, it seems to me, a rather problematic war correspondent insofar as he was perhaps a little too keen to become personally involved in the fighting. This proclivity makes Steinbeck's war-time experience unusual. You see, the nature of modern – even total – warfare suggests that most soldiers see very little 'action', in part because each front-line combatant depends upon the existence of a huge logistical operation that is designed around the need to feed, house, arm, transport, pay and, where necessary, nurse the front-line combatant. Most soldiers therefore tend to be involved in driving, cooking, cleaning and building rather than shooting. In contrast, war correspondents tend always to be 'in the thick of it' and tend always to be 'at the front' (even if most do not fight) because their editors demand good stories, and 'good stories' are defined in this context as being 'where the fighting is'. Yet despite the fact that Steinbeck had 'been where the action is' and despite the fact that he had actively participated in night raids on enemy positions, he chose not to place himself within his text. Introducing an edited collection of his war reporting, Steinbeck ([1959] 1990) discusses this choice. He confesses:

> All of us developed our coy little tricks with copy. Reading these old pieces I recognize one of mine. I never admitted having seen anything myself. In describing a scene I invariably put it in the mouth of someone else … It was the style to indicate that you were afraid all the time. I guess I was really afraid, but the style was there too. I think this was also designed to prove how brave the soldiers were. And the soldiers were just exactly as brave and as cowardly as anyone else.
>
> (7–8)

Steinbeck makes two rather important points here. First, he reminds us that as we attempt to change how people think, feel and act we are seldom usefully cast as the heroes of our own tales: No one likes a show-off! So if you need to extol the virtues and achievements of a special individual it is, I suggest, better not to claim personal responsibility for these endeavours.

Second, Steinbeck makes it clear that as a 'war reporter' he was not a simple chronicler of events. Indeed, it is clear that Steinbeck continued to regard himself as a storyteller, and so felt able – within practical and ethical limits – to change and embellish events to produce a desired outcome or, more plainly, a propaganda effect.

Given Steinbeck's guidance as to the ways and means of war reporting it may be useful to reflect upon the ways in which you cast your tales and the manner in which you frame your narratives. For example, you might ask yourself:

Who are the heroes of my tales?
Do these heroes usefully reflect the demographics of my workforce?
Do these heroes reflect or usefully project my company's ethos?

Equally you should ask yourself:

What do the heroes of my tales actually, say, think and do?
Are the heroes of my tales truly worthy?
Do my heroes acknowledge plurality?
Do my heroes make sound ethical choices?

Finally you might ask yourself:

Do I personally model the conduct of the heroes represented in my tales?
When tested do I reflect the very best of the heroes represented in my narratives?

5 Are my tales bland?

Epic stories dominate the tales that are published on the business of management. In these stories a handsome, dedicated, strong and gifted individual sets off, for example, on a quest to turn around a failing organization (see Collins and Rainwater 2005) and, along the way, overcomes trials and ordeals that would break the spirit of a normal human.

I don't know about your preferences but I do not really enjoy these stories. I prefer my 'heroes' to have more discernibly human qualities, by which I mean that I like my heroes to have flaws and imperfections.[2] I also find that I prefer the comic story-form. And you – as a would-be storyteller – should do too because in my experience it is the comic story-form that circulates most readily and most freely in organized settings. Given this, my fifth observation is designed to encourage you to adjust your default storytelling mode.

Comic tales travel freely and rapidly throughout organizations. Consequently comic stories are, it seems to me, readily sustained in the organization's collective memory. Given this, could you find some means of wrapping your message, your aspiration, within a comic narrative?

Could you use comic tales to disarm your political opponents?

Could laughter be brought to bear on forms of action that you would oppose?

Orwell ([1941] 1982) captures this latter point rather well. Writing during the darkest days of World War II he suggests that the English would never embrace a fascist junta because the sight of soldiers goose-stepping along the Mall[3] would reduce the population to laughter!

Höpfl (1995) offers a more contemporary if slightly risqué analysis. Thus she suggests that, in common with other masculine projections, the epic story-form cannot withstand even a modest snigger!

Studying 'peasant politics', Scott (1987) echoes Höpfl's warning. He suggests that laughter and mockery are weapons of the weak. We should add, however that these remain powerful weapons. As you construct your stories of change and worthwhile endeavour you should, I suggest, cultivate tales that laugh with others. Those in positions of power who cannot laugh *with* may soon find themselves laughed at!

6 Is my storytelling overly vulnerable to revision and contestation?

To tell a tale and to have this believed, enjoyed and repeated you will need to add detail, texture and colour to your narrative. Add too much detail, however, and you risk converting your story into a history which will invite factual verification. So when you announce a story you must recognise that in so doing you will need to tip-toe a route within and around narrative forms. Allow me to tease out this complex and rather testing requirement.

My friend became a photographer at the tender age of ten. Actually that is not quite true. Kids do not become photographers. Not even prodigious kids. Child protégés do maths. They do science. They do not – for some reason – become photographers at the age of ten. But they can become fascinated by 'the visual' and may at that point choose to embark upon a spiritual journey that will nourish a lifelong obsession with photography. This is what happened to my friend in his grandfather's garage in the summer of 1974.

Colin – my friend – was as usual enjoying a summer break at the home of his grandparents. One day while he was eating lunch Colin's grandfather dispatched him from the table to fetch the ice cream that was stored in a chest freezer in the garage.

For this tale to work we need to accept that ice cream often needs to thaw a little before it can be served. We also need to establish a few things that are important to the success of our tale. We need to establish, for example, that the garage belonging to Colin's grandfather is, quite unlike mine, tidy and well-ordered. Furthermore we need to be clear that this garage is, not just tidy, but clean and with white, painted, interior walls. Other elements of the story matter less to the integrity of the tale, however. You may, for example, choose to cast Colin's grandfather as a 'grumpy grandpa' or you may elect to cast him as a doting, kindly, individual with a warm heart full of sage advice and pockets packed with patriarchal mints. Generally I choose the latter option, but in truth the tale works however we cast the grandfather.

The garage belonging to Colin's grandpa had a direct connection to the house and could be entered – as I tell it – via a door in the utility room. The main entrance to the garage was, however, a metal door of the up-and-over type. This metal door was, it seems, in good order but had sustained some very minor damage. It had a hole in it; a hole about the size of a grain of sand. And, on this bright sunny day, light was streaming through the tiny hole to produce – on the clean, white, painted wall – a vivid colour image of the outside world. At that moment the garage changed and so did Colin. The garage became a pin-hole camera and Colin, enchanted by the image on the wall, became a (proto)photographer.

The story of Colin's epiphany could conclude at this point. We now have our photographer. But you could extend the tale. You could have Colin's photographic impulse nurtured by the kindly grandfather who has entered the garage to find out what is delaying the ice cream. Alternatively you could have Colin become a photographer despite the dismissive tone of his grumpy grandpa. Depending upon the purpose you wish to pursue you can choose from a range of options. I have, for example, kept faith with the bare facts of the tale insofar as the characters are all male. However I could envisage other circumstances when I might, for example, choose to construct a relationship between a special girl and the grandmother who acted as the midwife at the birth of this little photographer. But to keep the faith of the audience you will need to add colour and texture to the tale. And there is, I suggest, one single factual detail that you simply cannot omit or get wrong. If you omit or misrepresent this single fact the tale may collapse around you, because someone in your audience will surely possess this knowledge and may use it to interrupt your tale and, worse, to challenge the veracity of your whole narrative.

What is this fact? It is a small but important matter: Pinhole cameras produce inverted images. So as you frame Colin, or Hannah or Mary or Rajesh enraptured by the image of the outside world that has been – by the magic of physics – projected on to Grandpa's (or Grandma's) garage wall do be sure to point out that the earth and the sky, and Mr MacFarlane's Ford, and Mrs Smith's washing, and the Patel children playing in the street have all been turned upside down.

Plainly, facts matter.[4] But you need to make sure that you do not allow 'facts' (and the pedants who act as the self-appointed guardians of fact) to dominate your tale. Load your story, unnecessarily, with fact and it will transform from being a 'poetic tale' to become instead a 'report'.

Greatbatch and Clark (2005), despite the conceptual and methodological limitations of their study, remain keenly aware of this issue. They suggest that, in their seminar performances, gurus carefully frame their storytelling in order to forestall the interruptions of those who would, through a pointed interjection, seek to convert a 'story' into a 'report'. Thus Greatbatch and Clark suggest that management's gurus avoid saying things like:

> 'Wang Laboratories had a structure that was quite unlike any other and acted to foster innovation.'[5]

because they are aware that someone in the audience might respond:

> 'Well I worked ten years for Wang and what you are suggesting is baloney.'

Instead the authors suggest that gurus will often choose to disguise the identity of the organizations they are discussing:

> 'A well known, and well-regarded, organization for which I provided consultancy services had a remarkable structure that ...'

Foxboro, a company discussed in *In Search of Excellence* (Peters and Waterman 1982), perhaps unwittingly demonstrates another means by which organizational storytelling may be safeguarded against unhelpful revision. In this instance, however, the protection is provided not by anonymity but by institutionalisation.

As Peters and Waterman (1982) tell the tale, Foxboro was, in the late 1970s, a company in trouble. A 'high tech' company, Foxboro had bet its future on a key technological development but had been unable to bring this to market. In desperation, key personnel began to put in working days which stretched long into the night. Until one fateful evening when, just as all seemed lost, a key scientist managed to construct a working prototype of the long-sought-after innovation. Relieved and flushed with success, the scientist rushed from his laboratory in order to find another soul so that, together, they might share and give thanks for this breakthrough.

When I tell this tale I like to paint a (verbal) picture of the scientist, flushed with success, rushing from his laboratories along a dimly lit corridor; an unbuttoned lab coat flapping in his wake. Taking up the story, Peters and Waterman (1982) tell us that our flushed scientist made it to the company president's office where he outlined the features of the working prototype that would save the company.

Typically I place the president in a large, comfortable and stylishly appointed office when I recount these events. I allow the scientist to barge in to the office (it seems sensible to assume that the assistant to the president left for home some hours ago, and in any case allowing the scientist to enter unannounced adds to the drama). Furthermore, I like to suggest that the office is in shadow save for the small pool of light produced by a desk lamp.

Commenting on the events that will unfold in this setting, Peters and Waterman (1982) tell us that the president found the scientist's prototype to be both useful and elegant. Perhaps unsurprisingly, therefore, the president felt that he should – there and then – produce some tangible means of recognising the scientist's company-saving achievement. Indeed, Peters and Waterman tells us that, during this interaction, the company president began rifling his desk in an attempt to find a suitable token. At this point, when I perform the tale, I have the president take an inventory as he considers his options.

What can I give him? A paper knife? No.
A stapler? Stupid idea!
My lamp? No. Even more stupid. Idiot!
My Mont Blanc pen? No, better not, that was a graduation gift from Granny.

Taking up the tale again, Peters and Waterman tell us that while rifling the contents of his desk the president discovered a plump, yellow banana, a leftover from lunch. Relieved, he snatched the banana from the drawer thrust it into the hands of the now slightly bewildered scientist and announced something along the lines of: 'Great job. You've saved the company. Have a banana.'

Discussing the significance of this tale, Peters and Waterman (1982) suggest that it has become a part of Foxboro's folklore. Furthermore they suggest that the story has become institutionalised, and so protected to some degree from revision because those who would make a contribution to the company have an exemplar to emulate and when they do so their endeavours are rewarded with a coveted 'golden banana' lapel pin.

Given the Foxboro experience it seems sensible to suggest that when you have found a story that produces useful managerial outcomes you should take steps to protect its core narrative. To this end you might find it useful to call to mind a story that you find productive, and ask:

What steps might I take now to prevent my story being rewritten in a non-productive manner?

If your company has an award, what steps have you taken to craft stories around it? Indeed, you might ask yourself:

What can I do to make the award and the tales which surround it special?

Finally you should ask:

What might I do now to protect the prize (and the tale) from being devalued?

Remember: It is the person with the best, not the most stories who will define the future!

And with thoughts of the future in mind we now turn to retrace our steps.

Notes

1 I would, in truth, look in vain for such a place. Few modern universities have communal, social, space that is set aside for the exclusive use of staff members. But I must be allowed the odd poetic flourish!

2 Braddon (1956) offers a very human biography of Leonard Cheshire. Cheshire was an RAF pilot during World War II. He flew more than 100 combat missions. He was decorated many times and was awarded the VC for his uncommon bravery. He was a hero. But Braddon's account of Cheshire is unlike many modern biographies and is quite unlike most modern managerial biographies because it makes it plain that Cheshire was an unlikely hero. Unlike cinematic representations of James Bond, for example, Cheshire was not apparently blessed with great physical or mental talents. He was a limited and unenthusiastic sportsman. He was also a diffident and at times delinquent student. Indeed he was by his own admission a poor pilot who was rather fearful of heights. Despite these aspects of his character, however, Cheshire led an elite squadron and pioneered, at great personal risk, a widely adopted system of precision bombing. And perhaps more importantly, Braddon makes it plain that in the post-war period Cheshire – the efficient warrior – selflessly devoted himself to the care of the elderly, the disabled and the infirm. Cheshire seems to me a man with properly human qualities; a man deserving of honour and respect. A flawed human but a rather perfect hero.

3 This is of course the road in central London that runs from Buckingham Palace to Trafalgar Square.

4 Forrester (1956) captures the tensions associated with the narration of events and process, and in so doing offers a rationale for the exercise of 'poetic

licence'. Introducing his biography of R. S. Tuck (a British fighter pilot who was decorated for bravery during World War II) Forrester offers the following: 'There are no fictitious characters in this book, but there are a few fictitious names. It seems to me that so long after the war it would be needlessly cruel to reawaken anguished memories for the families of those Royal Air Force men who did not die quickly or cleanly, or who died stupidly; those who contracted unpleasant diseases or suffered extreme hardship in Nazi prison camps or "on the run"; the one or two who weakened and failed their comrades ... So I have changed the names, but not the facts. The facts are part of the story' (1956: 6, ellipses in original).

5 I have chosen Wang Laboratories in this illustration for two reasons. First it featured in *In Search of Excellence*. Second and more importantly, it is no longer trading.

6   Concluding comments

In this little book I have offered critical reflections and – I trust – thoughtful guidance on the practices and pitfalls of storytelling at work. At a general level I have traced the increasing academic and practitioner interest in storytelling, and I have attempted to provoke reflection on the often unacknowledged problems associated with the special form of persuasive talk that is organizational storytelling. To secure an understanding of organizational storytelling that you might 'put to work' I have examined the essence of the poetic tale and the important debates that persist as to the nature, function and capabilities of organizational storytelling. Reviewing the academic debates which should shape our appreciation of the politics and processes of organizational storytelling, I have sought to contextualise my analysis. I have, therefore, offered an account of the nature of management which analyses the nature of managerial control *and* its inherent limitations.

Noting the extent to which managerial accounts of storytelling build and depend upon sensegiving narratives, I have suggested that the impulse to direct others through stories is, at root, a reaction to the inherent limits of managerial control. After all, if shouting at people and threatening them had worked as motivational tools we would not have accepted 'scientific management' as a useful innovation. And if money had represented a sufficient inducement to hard work we would not have embraced 'human relations' approaches to management (Thompson and McHugh 1990; Huczynski 1993).

Observing that sensegiving perspectives assume that storytelling offers practitioners (a) a reliable means of animating employees, and (b) a useful method for reorienting their concerns, we have countered that stories, when viewed from a sensemaking perspective, actually provide employees with a basis for resistance. Yet all is not lost, since sensemaking accounts of storytelling also offer managers a source of local understanding; intelligence in any sense of the term.

Through our reflections on sensemaking we have attempted to deflate the egos of those who assume that organizational storytelling represents a panacea. Yet I cannot ignore the fact that stories do, often, move me in surprising ways. And I cannot pretend that I do not actually expect supermarket employees to offer a smile and good service. So in an attempt to acknowledge the sensemaking power of storytelling, the limits of managerial sensegiving and the inconsistent currents that so often guide thought and action, I have outlined six questions, or more properly, six sets of questions and observations, designed to promote talk and, yes, action on storytelling. These questions are 'critical-practical' in nature: They recognise the need for social co-operation within contexts which are nonetheless marked by political inequality. These questions also note the emotional nature of our organizational endeavours and the consequent need which managers have to secure emotional bonds. These characteristics, these foundational elements of our analysis, make our review of managerial talk distinctive because they recognise the underlying conflicts that structure our experience of work, the anxieties that are generated in and through working, and the emotional appeals and connections that can, however temporarily, overwrite these limitations.

What you do with now my words and reflections is up to you. The storyteller is, after all, always at the mercy of his or her audience!

I hope, of course, that my little book and my carefully chosen and crafted tales will move you to think and to talk about storytelling. Indeed, I hope that you will now accept and understand that talk is central to managerial work. Furthermore, I hope that you will act upon this knowledge in a manner that recognises the ways in which organizational sensemaking might challenge and respond to your storytelling.

Finally it is worth noting that I remain hopeful that my reflections on storytelling at work might actually encourage you to project *new narratives of working*; stories which embrace plurality; stories which construct and allow new forms of organizational membership.

In closing, therefore, I offer a final observation: Few of us are natural storytellers. Indeed, in my experience those who truly think themselves natural raconteurs tend to be crushing bores. Few people I know can, in an organizational context, spontaneously craft and render a tale that will move people and in so doing *get things done*. So if your storytelling is to qualify as purposeful talk, if it is to do something meaningful within your workplace, you will, I suggest, need to choose your tales carefully and, perhaps more importantly, you must seek out opportunities to rehearse and to refine your craft.

Of course I cannot guarantee that you will secure managerial success through storytelling. The organized world is too complex and too pluralistic to allow me to offer this indemnity. In closing, what I will venture is this: your plans and your ventures will surely fail if you cannot insinuate your ideas and your ambitions usefully in the company of others. So, if you hope to enjoy success in management you have no option but to embrace the power of talk in organizations.

Bibliography

Abercrombie, N., Hill, S. and Turner, B. (1994) *The Penguin Dictionary of Sociology*, Penguin: Harmondsworth.

Adorisio, A. L. M. (2009) *Storytelling in Organizations: From Theory to Empirical Research*, Palgrave Macmillan: Basingstoke.

Aristotle (1965) *The Politics*, trans. T. S. Dorsch. Penguin: London.

Barden, T. E. (ed.) (2012) *Steinbeck in Vietnam: Dispatches from the War*, University of Virginia Press: Charlottesville and London.

Bendix, R. ([1956] 1963) *Work and Authority in Industry*, Wiley: New York.

Benjamin, W. (1999) *Illuminations*, trans. H. Zorn. Pimlico: London.

Beynon, H. (1979) *Working for Ford*, Penguin: Harmondsworth.

Boje, D. (1991) 'The Storytelling Organization: A Study of Performance in an Office Supply Firm', *Administrative Science Quarterly* 36: 106–126.

Boje, D. (2001) *Narrative Methods for Organizational and Communication Research*, Sage: London.

Boje, D., Alvarez, R. and Schooling, B. (2001) 'Reclaiming Story in Organization: Narratologies and Action Sciences', in Westwood, R. and Linstead, S. (eds) *The Language of Organization*, Sage: London.

Boltanski, L. and Chiapello, E. (2007) *The New Spirit of Capitalism*, trans. Gregory Elliot. Verso: London.

Bott, G. (ed.) ([1958] 1985) *George Orwell: Selected Writings*, Heinemann: London.

Braddon, R. (1956) *Cheshire V.C.*, Companion Book Club: London.

Brown, A. D. (2000) 'Making Sense of Inquiry Sensemaking', *Journal of Management Studies* 37(1): 45–75.

Brown, A. D. (2003) 'Authoritative Sensemaking in a Public Inquiry', *Organization Studies* 25(1): 95–112.

Brown, A. D. (2005) 'Making Sense of the Collapse of Barings Bank', *Human Relations* 58(12): 1579–1604.

Brown, A. D. and Jones, M. (2000) 'Honourable Members and Dishonourable Deeds: Sensemaking, Impression Management and Legitimation in the "Arms to Iraq Affair"', *Human Relations* 53(5): 655–689.

Brown, G. (2010) *Beyond the Crash: Overcoming the First Crisis of Globaliza-tion*, Simon and Schuster: London.

Bryson, B. (2014) *One Summer: America 1927*, Black Swan: London.

Bunting, M. (2005) *Willing Slaves: How the Overwork Culture Is Ruling Our Lives*, Harper Perennial: London.

Butler, N. and Spoelstra, S. (2012) 'Your Excellency', *Organization* 19(6): 891–903.

Cathcart, T. and Klein, D. (2007) *Plato and a Platypus Walk into a Bar: Understanding Philosophy through Jokes*, Penguin: Harmondsworth.

Chia, R. and King, I. (1998) 'The Organizational Structuring of Novelty', *Organization* 5(4): 461–478.

Clark, T. and Greatbatch, D. (2002) 'Knowledge Legitimation and Affiliation Through Storytelling: The Example of Management Gurus', in Clark, T. and Fincham, R. (eds) *Critical Consulting: New Perspectives on the Man-agement Advice Industry*, Blackwell: Oxford.

Clark, T. and Greatbatch, D. (2003) 'Collaborative Relationships in the Crea-tion and Fashioning of Management Ideas: Gurus, Editors and Managers' in Kipping, M. and Engwall, L. (eds) *Management Consulting: Emergence and Dynamics of a Knowledge Industry*, Oxford University Press: Oxford.

Clark, T., Bhatanacharoen, P. and Greatbatch, D. (2012) 'Management Gurus as Celebrity Consultants' in Kipping, M. and Clark, T. (eds) *The Oxford Handbook of Management Consulting*, Oxford University Press: Oxford.

Cockburn, A. (1991) 'Street Children: Victims of Multiple Abuse', Unpub-lished paper presented at the South African Society for the Prevention of Child Abuse and Neglect conference, Durban.

Collins, D. (1997) 'Knowledge Work or Working Knowledge: Ambiguity and Confusion in the Analysis of the "Knowledge Age"', *Employee Relations* 19(1): 38–50.

Collins, D. (1998) *Organizational Change: Sociological Perspectives*, Routledge: London.

Collins, D. (2000) *Management Fads and Buzzwords: Critical-practical Per-spectives*, Routledge: London.

Collins, D. (2007) *Narrating the Management Guru: In Search of Tom Peters*, Routledge: London.

Collins, D. (2008) 'Has Tom Peters Lost the Plot? A Timely Review of a Celebrated Management Guru' *Journal of organizational Change Manage-ment* 21(3): 315–334.

Collins, D. (2012a) 'Women Roar: "The Women's Thing" in the Storywork of Tom Peters', *Organization* 19(4): 405–424.

Collins, D. (2012b) 'Management Fashion', in Boje, D., Burnes, B. and Hassard, J. (eds) *The Routledge Companion to Organizational Change*, Routledge: Abingdon.

Collins, D. (2013) 'In Search of Popular Management: Sensemaking, Sensegiving and Storytelling in the Excellence Project', *Culture and Organization*, 19(1): 42–61.

Collins, D. and Rainwater, K. (2005) 'Managing Change at Sears: A Sideways Look at a Tale of Corporate Transformation', *Journal of Organizational Change Management* 18(1): 16–30.

Collins, D., Dewing, I. and Russell, P. (2015) 'Between Maxwell and Micawber: Plotting the Failure of the Equitable Life', *Accounting and Business Research* 45(6–7): 715–737.

Cunliffe, A. (2011) 'Crafting Qualitative Research: Morgan and Smircich 30 Years On', *Organizational Research Methods* 14(4): 647–673.

Czarniawska, B. (1997) *Narrating the Organization: Dramas of Institutional Identity*, University of Chicago Press: Chicago, IL.

Czarniawska, B. (1999) *Writing Management: Organization Theory as a Literary Genre*, Oxford University Press: Oxford.

Deal, T. and Kennedy, A. (1982) *Corporate Cultures: The Rites and Rituals of Corporate Life*, Addison-Wesley: Reading, MA.

De Cock, C. and Hipkin, I. (1997) 'TQM and BPR: Beyond the Beyond Myth', *Journal of Management Studies* 34(5): 659–675.

Denning, S. (2001) *The Springboard: How Storytelling Ignites Action in Knowledge-era Organizations*, Routledge: Abingdon.

Dickens, C. [1841] (1922) *A Christmas Carol*, Cecil Palmer: London.

Double, O. (2005) *Getting the Joke: The Inner Workings of Stand-up Comedy*, Methuen: London.

Dunlap, A. and Andelman, B. (1997) *Mean Business: How I Save Bad Companies and Make Good Companies Great*, Fireside: New York.

Economist, 15 May 2008.

Edwards, P. K. (1986) *Conflict at Work*, Blackwell: Oxford.

Esler, G. (2012) *Lessons from the Top: How Successful Leaders Tell Stories to Get Ahead and Stay There*, Profile Books: London.

Fayol, H. (1949) *General and Industrial Management*, Pitman: London.

Forrester, L. (1956) *Fly For Your Life: The Story of Wing Commander Robert Stanford Tuck*, Panther: London.

Fox, A. (1985) *History and Heritage: Social Origins of the British Industrial Relations System*, Allen & Unwin: London.

Gabriel, Y. (1995) 'The Unmanaged Organization: Stories, Fantasies and Subjectivity', *Organization Studies* 16(3): 477–501.

Gabriel, Y. (1998) 'Same Old Story or Changing Stories? Folkloric, Modern and Postmodern Mutations', in Grant, D., Keenoy, T. and Oswick, C. (eds) *Discourse and Organization*, Sage: London.

Gabriel, Y. (2000) *Storytelling in Organizations: Facts, Fictions and Fantasies*, Oxford University Press: Oxford.

Gabriel, Y. (2004) 'Narratives, Stories and Texts', in Grant, D., Hardy, C., Oswick, C. and Putnam, L. (eds) *The Sage Handbook of Organizational Discourse*, Sage: London.

Geneen, H. and Moscow, A. (1986) *Managing*, Grafton Books: London.

Gioia, D. A. and Chittipeddi, K. (1991) 'Sensemaking and Sensegiving in Strategic Change Initiation', *Strategic Management Journal* 12: 433–448.

Gourevitch, P. (1998) *We Wish to Inform You That Tomorrow We Will Be Killed With Our Families: Stories from Rwanda*, Picador: London.

Grady, J. [1974] (2015) *Six Days of the Condor*, No Exit Press: Harpenden.

Greatbatch, D., and Clark, T. (2005) *Management Speak: Why We Listen to What Management Gurus Tell Us*, Routledge: London.

Grint, K. (1994) 'Reengineering History: Social Resonances and Business Process Reengineering', *Organization* 1(1): 179–201.

Grint, K. (1997) 'TQM, BPR, JIT, and TLAs: Managerial Waves or Drownings', *Management Decision* 35(10): 731–738.

Groβ, C., Heusinkveld, S. and Clark, T. (2015) 'The Active Audience? Gurus, Management Ideas and Consumer Variability', *British Journal of Management* 51(1): 273–291.

Hales, C. (1993) *Management Through Organization: The Management Process, Forms of Organization and the Work of Managers*, Routledge: London.

Harris, A. ([1947] 2005) *Bomber Offensive*, Pen & Sword: Barnsley.

Harvey-Jones, J. (1994) *All Together Now*, Heinemann: London.

Höpfl, H. (1995) 'Organizational Rhetoric and the Threat of Ambivalence', *Studies in Culture, Organisations and Society* 1(2): 175–188.

Huczynski, A. A. (1993) *Management Gurus: What Makes Them and How to Become One*, Routledge: London.

Huczynski, A. A. and Buchanan, D. (2007) *Organizational Behaviour: An Introductory Text*, Financial Times/Prentice Hall: Harlow.

Jackson, B. (1996) 'Re-engineering the Sense of Self: The Managers and the Management Guru', *Journal of Management Studies* 33(5): 571–589.

Jackson, B. (2001) *Management Gurus and Management Fashions: A Dramatistic Inquiry*, Routledge: London.

Latour, B. (1987) *Science in Action*, Harvard University Press: Cambridge MA.

Lee, S. (2010) *How I Escaped My Certain Fate: The Life and Deaths of a Stand-up Comedian*, Faber and Faber: London.

Marchington, M. (2005) 'Employee Involvement: Patterns and Explanations', in Harley, B., Hyman, J. and Thompson, P. (eds) *Participation and Democracy at Work: Essays in Honour of Harvie Ramsay*, Palgrave Macmillan: Basingstoke.

Marshak, R. J. (1998) 'A Discourse on Discourse: Redeeming the Meaning of Talk', in Grant, D., Keenoy, T. and Oswick, C. (eds) *Discourse and Organization*, Sage: London.

Martin, J., Feldman, M. S., Hatch, M. J. and Sitkin, S. B. (1983) 'The Uniqueness Paradox in Organizational Stories', *Administrative Science Quarterly* 28: 438–453.

Middlebrook, M. (1985) The *Schweinfurt-Regensburg Mission: American Raids on 17th August 1943*, Cassell: London.

Middlebrook, M. and Everett, C. (1985) *The Bomber Command War Diaries*, Viking: London.

Mintzberg, H. (1973) *The Nature of Managerial Work*, Harper and Row: New York.

Orwell, G. ([1941] 1982) *The Lion and the Unicorn: Socialism and the English Genius*, Penguin: Harmondsworth.

Parini, J. (1994) *John Steinbeck: A Biography*, Heinemann: London.

Parker, M. and Thomas, R. (2011) 'What Is a Critical Journal?', *Organization* 18(4): 419–427.

Pascale, R. T. and Athos, A. G. ([1981]1986) *The Art of Japanese Management*, Sidgwick and Jackson: London.

Pattison, S. (1997) *The Faith of the Managers: When Management Becomes Religion*, Cassell: London.

Peters, T. (1988) *Thriving on Chaos: Handbook for a Management Revolution*, Pan: London.

Peters, T. and Austin, N. (1985) *A Passion for Excellence: The Leadership Difference*, Fontana: London.

Peters, T. and Waterman, R. (1982) *In Search of Excellence: Lessons from America's Best Run Companies*, Harper and Row: New York.

Ramsay, H. (1975) 'Research Note: Firms and Football Teams', *British Journal of Industrial Relations* 13(3): 396–400.

Ramsay, H. (1977) 'Cycles of Control', *Sociology* 11(3): 481–506.

Scott, J. C. (1987) *Weapons of the Weak: Everyday Forms of Peasant Resistance*, Yale University Press: New Haven CT.

Søderberg, A. (2003) 'Sensegiving and Sensemaking in an Integration Process: A Narrative Approach to the Study of an International Acquisition', in Czarniawska, B. and Gagliardi, P. (eds) *Narratives We Organize By*, John Benjamins: Amsterdam.

Steinbeck, J. ([1937] 1974) *Of Mice and Men*, Pan Books: London.

Steinbeck, J. ([1942] (1983) *The Moon Is Down*, Penguin: London.

Steinbeck, J. ([1959] 1990) *Once There Was a War*, Mandarin Paperbacks: London.

Thompson, E. P. ([1963] 1972) *The Making of the English Working Class*, Penguin: Harmondsworth.

Thompson, E. P. (1967) 'Time, Work-discipline and Industrial Capitalism', *Past and Present* 38: 56–97.

Thompson, P. and McHugh, D. (1990) *Work Organisations: A Critical Introduction*, Palgrave: Basingstoke.

Tietze, S., Cohen, L. and Musson, G. (2003) *Understanding Organizations through Language*, Sage: London.

Watson, T. (2001) *In Search of Management: Culture, Chaos and Control in Managerial Work*, Thomson Learning: London.

Weick, K. (1993) 'The Collapse of Sensemaking in Organizations: The Mann Gulch Disaster', *Administrative Science Quarterly* 38: 628–652.

Weick, K. (1995) *Sensemaking in Organizations*, Sage: London.

Wright, P. (1980) *On a Clear Day You Can See General Motors*, Sidgwick and Jackson: London.

Wright, P. (2000) *Tank: The Progress of a Monstrous War Machine*, Faber: London.

Wright, S. (1994) *Anthropology of Organizations*, Routledge: London.

Zuboff, S. (1988) *In the Age of the Smart Machine*, Heinemann: New York.

Index

management and 63, 67; narrative resources 55–6; *Star Wars* 55–6
Equitable Life 44–5
Esler, Gavin 21, 23, 24
Everett, Chris 37

facts 24, 50, 69–70, 73n4
Fayol, Henri 6, 7
Ford, Henry 9
Forrester, Larry 72–3n4
Foxboro 70–1

Gabriel, Yiannis 24, 29, 31–4 *passim*, 51, 55; 6F-factors 34, 37–45; essence of stories 49–50; Gabriel/ Boje comparison 26–7; poetic tropes 53–4; storywork and knowledge 26
Geneen, Harold 8
getting things done 6, 7, 9, 15, 18, 23, 75
Grady, James: *Six Days of the Condor* 43
Greatbatch, David 50–3, 63, 70
guru (management's gurus) 50, 51, 70; audience and 52; comic narratives and 63; 'guru theory' 1; storytelling in guru seminars 52–3

Harvard Business Review 25, 63
Hemingway, Ernest 27–8
hero 34, 47, 48, 53, 54, 55, 56, 66–7; human qualities and imperfections of 67, 72n2
Höpfl, Heather 68
Huczynski, Andrzej 1

Jackson, Brad 1–2
joke 5, 57; joke and philosophy 10–11n1; *see also* laughter

Klein, Daniel 10–11n1

labour power 7–8
laughter 5, 54, 58, 67–8; audience and 50, 52; *see also* joke
listener 51; *see also* audience

management/managing 3; action-orientation management 6;

complexity of 5, 6; as moral project 2, 10, 23; output-focused account of management 3, 6; scientific management 74; as social-political process 3, 6–7, 9; *see also* manager; managerial work
manager 8; American manager 13, 15; hierarchy 6; Japanese manager 13–14; story and 15; storytelling and 21; talk and 10, 12, 23; tasks of 6–7, 10; *see also* management/ managing; managerial work
managerial control 2, 7; limitations of 9–10, 74; as self-defeating 7, 9
managerial success: organizational storytelling and 2, 3, 76; purposeful talk and 12
managerial talk 2, 75; *see also* organizational storytelling
managerial work 3, 5–11, 75; as narrative endeavour 3; storytelling and 3, 23; *see also* management/ managing; manager
Martin, Joanne 51, 62–3
Maxwell, Robert 44, 60n2
MBWA (management by wandering around) 15
McKinsey 7-S model 13, *14*
Memphis Belle 37–8, 39, 43
Micawber, Wilkins 44, 45, 60n3
Middlebrook, Martin 37–8
Mintzberg, Henry 6–7

narrative 15, 18; contemporary management and 2; narrative monologue 28; narrative resources 4, 38, 39, 44, 49, 54–9; narrative types 30; new narratives of working 75; social life/social action and 18–19; 'story'/'narrative' distinction 24, 25, 26
Nike corporation 24–5

opinion 3, 29, **31**; characteristics of 32
organizational storytelling 12, 74; academy 24, 51–3; decline of 16–7; importance of 2, 27, 61; managerial success and 2, 3, 76; managerial talk 2; organizational storyworld

defining our sense of self and relationships with others 15; earworm/
earwig 21, 22; essence of 49–51;
fragile and 'polysemic' quality of
24; as generator and creator of
meaning 24; good story 19, 26, 66,
72; manager and 15; managerial
success and 2; shared story 16;
'story'/'narrative' distinction 24,
25, 26; 'story'/'report' distinction
30, 37, 44; storywork and knowledge 26; translation of 24; *see also*
6F-factors; antenarrative; shaping
thoughts and actions; tale
storyteller 4, 72, 75; audience and 51,
75; report and 30; story, defined
not by form but by proclamation 51
storytelling: common purpose and
15, 23; importance of 15–16; manager and 21; managerial work and
3, 23; nature of 51; as purposeful
talk 12; *see also* organizational
storytelling
storytelling, deductive/inductive division 3–4, 30; deductive approach
53; inductive approach 50, 53
storytelling practice 4, 59, 61, 62, 74;
Are my storytelling practices
exclusionary? 63–4
Summer Holiday 39, 59–60n1
symbolism 15, 31, 32, 27, 50

tale: terse tale 27–8; *see also* comic
tale; epic tale; poetic tale; romantic
tale; story; tragic tale
talk: denigration/devaluation of 2;
emotion and 10; importance of 10,
15–16, 75; manager and 10, 12, 23;
persuasive talk 2, 10, 74; power of
talk 1, 4, 51, 53, 76; purposeful
talk 10, 12, 75; 'talk is cheap' 1, 5
'talk' and 'action' 1, 2, 23; talk as
subordinate to action 2, 3; You
talk the talk but can you walk the
walk? 2–3, 5; *see also* shaping
thoughts and actions
texture and colour 49, 68–9
Thompson, Edward Palmer 9
Three Days of the Condor 43
Tiananmen Square, reports on 45–9;
context 45; Deng Xiaoping 47–8;
PLA 46, 47; Tank Man 45, 46–9;
see also report
tragic tale 4, 35, 54; *Inside Job* 58–9;
narrative resources 58–9

Wang Laboratories 70, 73n5
Waterman, Robert: *In Search of
Excellence* 12, 13,
14–15, 70–1, 73n5
Weick, Karl 3, 18–20, 25; *see also*
sensemaking process
Wright, Patrick 47, 48

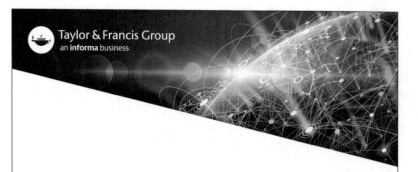